# ARTICULATING WITH DIFFICULTY

### New BERA Dialogues

The BERA Dialogues series was created by the British Educational Research Association in order to facilitate the publication of collections of high quality educational research papers on particular themes. Paul Chapman Publishing took over publication of the series – New BERA Dialogues – for BERA in 1995. To be included in the series, collections should normally meet the criteria of

(a) being internally coherent, with all the papers addressing a clearly identified theme;
(b) consisting of scholarly papers, with at least most of those in any collection being of a standard that would make them acceptable to leading journals such as the *British Educational Research Journal*;
(c) being of interest to the international educational research community.

Among appropriate starting points for editions of Dialogues can be collections of papers delivered at a BERA Day Conference or in a symposium at the BERA Annual Conference. While most collections in the series have been of papers reporting research, not all editions need be of that kind. For example, collections of papers debating methodological, political or ethical issues in educational research could be highly appropriate for the series.

Paul Chapman Publishing meet annually with the series editor, currently Donald McIntyre, to agree on a set of new editions which will meet the above criteria and which will be commercially viable. Donald McIntyre (School of Education, University of Cambridge) or Marianne Lagrange of PCP welcome suggestions for additions to the series from potential editors.

# ARTICULATING WITH DIFFICULTY

## RESEARCH VOICES IN INCLUSIVE EDUCATION

*edited by*

*Peter Clough and Len Barton*

*New Bera Dialogues*

P·C·P

Paul Chapman
Publishing Ltd

Paul Chapman Publishing Ltd
A SAGE Publications company
6 Bonhill Street
London EC2A 4PU

SAGE Publications Inc.
2455 Teller Road
Thousand Oaks, California 91320

SAGE Publications India Pvt Ltd
32, M-Block Market
Greater Kailash-I
New Delhi 110 048

**British Cataloguing in Publication Data**

Articulating with difficulty – research voices in special
    education. – (New BERA dialogues)
    1. Special education 2. Special education – Research
    I. Clough, Peter II. Barton
    371.9'072

ISBN 1 853964123 (hbk)
ISBN 1 853964107 (pbk)

**Library of Congress catalog card number**

Typeset by Dorwyn Ltd, Hampshire
Printed and bound by Atheneum Press, Tyne & Wear
A B C D E F  3 2 1 0 9 8

# CONTENTS

# SERIES EDITOR'S PREFACE

This book appears in the *New BERA Dialogues* series at a time when loud, if not very informed or thoughtful, voices are being raised about *bias* in educational research. It is therefore a very timely book, not least in that it addresses the issue of bias in an informed, intelligent and highly thought-provoking way. The book's primary concern is to contribute to our understanding of inclusive education and to discuss the kind of contribution that research can usefully make to such understanding; and in my view it does that very well. In its focus on the concept of *voice*, however, its implications are much wider. The field of inclusive education is, almost necessarily, an emotive one, and certainly one in which the need for insightful understanding and for rigorous collection and examination of evidence cannot be detached from educational values and political positions. It therefore offers a very appropriate arena within which to explore either the crude concept of *bias* or, as the editors and authors of this book wisely prefer, the potentially much more subtle concept of *voice*. Thus in this book we not only have some excellent examples of researchers discussing and reporting their work from clearly stated value and political positions, but more fundamentally we have valuable explorations of the complexities of doing this in principled and valid ways. The significance of *voice* as a concept, with the implications of a speaker and also of an audience and an occasion, with questions about whether voices are heard and also about whether they are authentic and valid, and – as Peter Clough says in the final chapter – the idea that 'above all . . . "voice" is always *contestable*', is very helpfully explored from a number of perspectives. Most fundamental of all for educational researchers is the question of the claims that we make in relation to representing voices other than our own. I found this is a very helpful and interesting book to read and I am sure that the same will be true for other educational researchers.

*Donald McIntyre*

# NOTES ON CONTRIBUTORS

Alan Dyson is Professor of Special Needs Education, Co-Director of the Special Needs Research Centre and Director for Research in the Department of Education, University of Newcastle upon Tyne. He has published and researched widely in the field of special needs education, and is a member of the National Advisory Group on Special Educational Needs which is working on the implementation of the SEN Green Paper. His recent publications with colleagues at Newcastle include *New Directions in Special Needs* (1997, Cassell) and *Theorising Special Education* (1998, Routledge). He has been at Newcastle University since 1988. Prior to that, he spent 13 years as a teacher in special and mainstream schools in Newcastle and elsewhere in the north-east of England.

Patricia Potts is a member of the Inclusive Education group in the School of Education at the Open University, Milton Keynes, and has co-authored a wide range of multi-media courses for undergraduate, postgraduate and professional audiences. Before joining the Open University, Patricia worked for the Inner London Education Authority. Her research interests include the comparative study of barriers to learning, especially in China, Hong Kong and Europe, oral history and education, histories of special education and teacher education, architecture and learning and theories of child development.

Len Barton is Professor of Education at the University of Sheffield and the founder and editor of the journal *Disability and Society*.

John Swain is a Reader in Disability Studies at the University of Northumbria, and contributed to the production of a number of Open University courses in disability studies. He has been a member of a number of research teams working with people with learning difficulties.

Sally French is a part-time Lecturer in the Department of Health Studies at Brunel University and also works as a physiotherapist with adults with learning disabilities. Her major interest is in the field of Disability Studies where she has written and edited various books. She was also involved in writing the Open University course *Disabling Society – Enabling Interventions.*

Jenny Corbett is Senior Lecturer in Special Education at the University of London Institute of Education. She has taught in schools, further education and in higher education. During her professional career, she has worked with students who experience a wide range of disabilities which include autism, physical and learning disabilities. The issues of inclusive education and the language of research voices are a particular interest and are reflected in two recent solo-authored books, *Bad-Mouthing: the language of special needs* (Falmer Press, 1996) and *Special Educational Needs in the Twentieth Century: a cultural analysis* (Cassell, 1998).

Professor Hazel Bines is responsible for teacher education in the Faculty of Health, Social Work and Education at the University of Northumbria. Previously she was Deputy Head of the School of Education and lectured in special educational needs at Oxford Brookes University. Her research interests include policy development and sociological perspectives in relation to special educational needs and she has published books, book chapters and journal articles on a range of issues. She has taught in primary, secondary and special schools.

John Kaye is a Senior Lecturer in Education in the Faculty of Health, Social Work and Education at the University of Northumbria. He is currently involved with both initial training and in-service courses for teachers, His research interests include the perspectives and experiences of teachers in relation to special educational needs.

Following her PhD on *Gender and Option Choice in Two Rural Comprehensive Schools*, at Bristol University in 1988, Sheila Riddell worked as Research Fellow in the Department of Education, University of Edinburgh, on a project investigating the impact of the 1981 Education (Scotland) Act, on children with special education needs. From 1989 to 1996 she was employed at Stirling University and was given a chair in 1995. After a period as Dean of Arts and Social Science at Napier University, Sheila now holds the Strathclyde Region Chair of Disability Research in the Department of Social Policy and Social work at the University of Glasgow. She has researched and written extensively in the areas of special educational needs/disability and gender education. Publications include *Gender and the Politics of Curriculum Change* (Routledge, 1992) and *Policy, Practice and Provision for Children with Specific Learning Difficulties* (Avebury, 1995).

Heather Wilkinson is currently Research Fellow in the Centre for Dementia Research, University of Stirling. Prior to that, she worked as a Research Fellow on the ESRC project *The Meaning of the Learning Society for Adults with Learning Difficulties,* based at Glasgow University. Prior to this project Heather spent five years as a researcher in the Departments of Applied Social Science and Educational Research, Lancaster University, where she worked in the areas of integration of children with special educational needs, community development and family support, and community care. She also undertook a PhD on *The Process of Parental Choice for Mothers of Children with Special Needs.* Heather's research interests are adults with learning difficulties, The Learning Society, special educational needs/disability, gender and markets.

Stephen Baron is Senior Lecturer in the Department of Education, Glasgow University. He has researched in the area of learning difficulties, since 1980 and published *Community Normality and Difference: meeting special needs* (Aberdeen University Press, 1992). He held a research grant from Forth Valley Health Board from 1992–95 to develop auditing mechanisms for the care in the community for children referred by GPs and older people discharged from the Royal Scottish National Hospital. Currently completing the manuscript *Community and Control: Surveillance, Containment and the State* (Addison, Wesley and Longman).

Harry Daniels has taught in mainstream and special schools and units. He is currently Professor of Special Education and Educational Psychology at the University of Birmingham having previously worked at the Institute of Education, University of London. His current research interests are in gender and attainment in junior schools, peer support for teachers, emotional and behavioural difficulty and mental health. His is currently president of the Association of Workers for Children with Emotional and Behavioural Difficulties (AWCEBD) and the European Association of Special Education (EASE).

Dan Goodley recently completed a PhD at the University of Sheffield appraising self-advocacy in the lives of people with learning difficulties. Now a lecturer in critical psychology at Bolton Institute. Current research interests include narrative methods, critical psychology, social model of disability and the actions of disability activists with learning difficulties.

Peter Clough is a lecturer and member of the Inclusive Education Research Centre at the University of Sheffield. He has worked as a teacher in all phases of UK public education. His main research interest is in special and inclusive education as it is experienced by learners, parents, teachers and other realizers of policy; much of his writing is currently occupied with the possibilities of fiction and other narrative modes as a means of richly communicating these experiences. With Len Barton he was editor of *Making Difficulties: research and the construction of special educational need* (Paul Chapman Publishing 1995) and has also edited *Managing Inclusive Education: from policy to experience* (Paul Chapman Publishing, 1998).

# 1

# PROFESSIONAL INTELLECTUALS FROM POWERFUL GROUPS: WRONG FROM THE START?

## Alan Dyson

*Making Difficulties* (Clough and Barton, 1995b) is an important book because, for the first time so far as I am aware in the UK, it presents a substantial
and sustained attempt to take research in special needs education as problematic and to pose a series of challenges to the way that such research has
traditionally been conducted. In particular, it calls – directly or by implication
– for a new kind of research which is more closely aligned with the interests of,
and perhaps even controlled by, those disabled people who have previously
only been thought of as the 'subjects' of research. In so doing, *Making Difficulties* implies serious questions about the role of the 'professional intellectual'
in special needs education. Such professionals (amongst whom I count myself)
are those members of the academic community who may well have a personal
commitment to the interests of disabled people and/or other 'oppressed
groups', but whose research and whose stance towards special needs education
fails to reflect in any obvious way the principles and commitments advocated
in *Making Difficulties*.

In this chapter, therefore, I propose to explore the extent to which the
powerful critiques articulated by Clough and Barton's contributors leave any
space within which the professional intellectual can operate. In so doing, I shall
follow the editors' invitation to see the book as the product of a 'collective
voice' (Barton and Clough, 1995, p. 143), though only too conscious that such
a move risks doing violence to the subtleties and doubts of individual contributions. I shall justify this by suggesting that the complex positions delineated by
those contributions actually reflect to a greater or lesser extent a wider
movement in disability research and beyond towards what Oliver (1992a)

characterterises as 'emancipatory research'. Only by surfacing the assumptions underlying the apparent complexity of individual positions, I believe, is it possible both to realise the power of this critique of traditional research and to move beyond that critique to alternative positions.

## THE CRITIQUES

In introducing *Making Difficulties*, Clough and Barton assert that:

> Much of the research [on special educational needs] has been strongly influenced by positivist assumptions. This has legitimated a form of psychological and individual reductionism which views '. . . the problem which disabled people face as being caused by their own impairments' (Oliver, 1992[a], p. 108). Within this tradition there exists a powerful ideological role given to the discourse of objectivity (Zarb, 1992). (Clough and Barton, 1995a, pp. 3–4)

This concern to define a research position in contradistinction to positivist assumptions reflects both a wider 'paradigm dialogue' (Guba, 1990b) within educational research and a wider dissatisfaction with positivist assumptions in the field of special needs education (see, for instance, Skrtic, 1995). As Guba makes clear,

> The basic belief system of positivism is rooted in a *realist* ontology, that is, the belief that there exists a reality *out there*, driven by immutable natural laws. The business of science is to discover the 'true' nature of reality and how it 'truly' works. The ultimate aim of science is to *predict* and *control* natural phenomena. (Guba, 1990a, p. 19, emphases in original)

In terms of special needs education, these assumptions can be seen as translating into three tenets:

- Special educational needs are real (i.e. observable and objectively describable) phenomena in the world.
- The task of research is to describe, analyse and test interventions in those needs through a scientific process of investigation which is rule-bound, publicly testable and which therefore gives access to some final or provisional truth about special needs.
- The extent to which the researcher exists as social actor or research production is a social process is made irrelevant by the reality of the phenomena under investigation and the rule-bound, publicly testable nature of the investigative process.

In so far as *Making Difficulties* is indeed the product of a collective voice, that voice is engaged in a concerted attempt to critique these assumptions and to explore alternatives. Moreover, it is possible to identify a number of recurrent themes in that critique:

## The process of research production

This theme attacks the assumption that the social process of research production is made irrelevant by the rule-bound and testable nature of the investigation. It asserts that, not only is research production part of wider social processes, but those processes are characterised by the exercise of power and the workings of vested interest. These characteristics are most evident in policy-related research where powerful policy-makers are able to dictate the research agenda and to some extent shape research findings (see, for instance, the chapters by Fulcher and by Riddell, Brown and Duffield). However, they are also evident in the ways in which research production serves the interests of researchers themselves, in advancing their careers and/or maintaining their professional position.

The appropriate *response* to this situation is for researchers to become *reflexive* in their awareness of how they are enmeshed in these processes, for them to *struggle* against the undue exercise of power, and for them to *align* their researching with the interests of the less powerful rather than the more powerful (see Barton and Clough's chapter).

## The process of knowledge production

In her chapter, Anastasia Vlachou questions the assumption that photography (particularly the photographing of disabled people) has a purely 'objective function' (p. 116). Photography, she argues, is not merely a case of recording what is 'really there', but is a construction of a particular image of what is 'there' – an image which then determines how that which is photographed is subsequently perceived. The photographing of disabled people has tended to be used to present them as 'dependent, socially dead, miserable, non-functional creatures that provoke feelings of pity, fear and guilt' (p. 117), largely because disabled people themselves have not been permitted to take control of photographic production.

Vlachou's arguments form part of a wider critique of research production. The research process, like the photographic process, cannot be assumed to generate or access something that can unequivocally be characterised as 'truth'. On the contrary, the research process actually constitutes the object of its inquiry both through the categories through which it seeks to understand that object and through the relationships it institutes between researcher and research subjects. Categories such as 'children with special educational needs' or 'people with disabilities' have the effect of reducing the richness and complexity of human lives to a few selected characteristics. Moreover, since those categories are determined by researchers, they effectively exclude the subjects of research from any participation in the construction of knowledge about themselves; they are instead constrained to be known simply in terms of the reductionist categories to which researchers allocate them (see Clough and Barton's introductory chapter).

The appropriate *response* to this situation seems to be that researchers have to search for means of constructing the subjects of their research which are not inherently reductionist. However, since any construction of one person by another is likely to be reductionist in effect, the subjects of research have themselves to *participate* in construction of knowledge about themselves (as, for instance, in Swain's chapter). This is frequently expressed in terms of letting the *voices* of research subject be heard through the research process. There seems to be a range of positions that can be adopted as to how this might be done, from simply paying close attention to what research subjects say about themselves (as in Hill's chapter), through to research which is conducted by disabled people on issues which they themselves see as significant (as in Peters' contribution).

## The process of researcher production

This critique is aimed at the assumption that the researcher as social actor, indeed, as 'self', is irrelevant to the research process. Researchers are themselves participants in and products of the social processes which underlie the production of research and knowledge. In so far as those processes are reductionist and oppressive, then researchers themselves may be unwitting oppressors, try as they may to disentangle themselves by taking heed of the two preceding critiques. Indeed, this unwitting oppression can beset even those researchers who are themselves members of the oppressed group of research subjects, since they too are, of course, implicated in and subject to wider social processes.

The *response* to this situation seems to be for the researcher to undergo a sort of personal purification and reconstruction through which s/he *struggles* to disentangle her/himself from those oppressive structures which have been internalised (as in Bines' chapter). For researchers who are not themselves members of the oppressed group which is 'being researched', this may involve an attempt to establish 'authentic' relationships with those subjects (as in the case of Swain), or indeed, in placing themselves as researchers at the disposal of research subjects, so that their inevitably oppressive individual identities can be subjugated. However, it does raise the possibility that, in an inherently oppressive society, those who are not themselves members of the oppressed group may not be able to replace their oppressive consciousnesses with the consciousness of the oppressed, and therefore that they have no legitimate place in the research process. It is, presumably, for this reason that Peters argues that '[t]he capability for change ultimately rests with the authentic voices of people with disabilities' (Peters, 1995, p. 73).

## VALIDITY AND *MAKING DIFFICULTIES*

At the heart of the critiques of positivist research articulated in *Making Difficulties* is a debate about the nature of validity, understood not as a technical matter but as the fundamental issue of how we access the 'truth' about disability or special educational needs, and who is capable of uncovering and uttering this 'truth'. The mistrust of what Riddell and her colleagues call 'the authoritative researcher voice' (Riddell, Brown and Duffield, 1995, p. 39) and the increased reliance on Peters' 'authentic voices of people with disabilities' in fact reflects a wider movement in the field of disability and special educational needs (see, for instance, Ballard, 1994, 1995; Barnes, 1992; Barton, 1994; Meekosha and Jakubowicz, 1996; Oliver, 1992a, 1992b) towards recognising the voices of disabled people themselves as the means whereby the 'truth' about disability comes to be articulated. This in turn reflects an attempt within emancipatory research and its variants to shift the former 'subjects' of research from the background to the foreground by enabling their voices to be heard and by handing over to them increasing control of the research process itself (see, for instance, Gitlin *et al.*, 1992; Kincheloe, 1991; McLaughlin and Tierney, 1993; Reason and Rowan, 1981a). Needless to say, the further such moves go in handing over research to the researched, the more problematic and marginal the role of the 'authoritative researcher voice' becomes. It may well be, indeed, that no space is left within which the professional intellectual can operate.

As many commentators have noted, the shift from positivism raises major issues about the notion of 'validity' which is so central to positivist research (see, for instance, Eisner, 1991; Guba, 1990a; Lincoln and Guba, 1985; Reason and Rowan, 1981b). So long as the world is seen as real and observable, then validity consists simply in following appropriate procedures to ensure that it is the reality of the world that is observed rather than any misleading appearances. However, when, as in much of *Making Difficulties*, the world is seen as constructed by the social actors who inhabit it, the question of validity becomes much more problematic. Put simply, whose construction of the world is the 'true' one, or, if all are to be taken as equally 'true', on what basis is mutual understanding to be reached and joint action undertaken?

One move which has been characteristic of emancipatory research and its variants is to exploit the potential for multiple constructions in order to subvert and critique those constructions which are currently dominant (Heron, 1988; Lather, 1986, 1994; LeCompte, 1993; Reason and Rowan, 1981b). Lather summarises this as an attempt to move discussion

> from the epistemological criteria of validity as a relation of correspondence between thought and its object to the generation of counterpractices of authority grounded in the crisis of representation. (1994, p. 40)

Put simply, where one 'version' of the truth has become hegemonic, it is the task of the researcher to seek out alternative versions which open up alternative possibilities for understanding and hence for action. What matters, therefore, is not whether a statement about the world is 'true' in the positivist sense, but whether it opens up these alternative possibilities. Lather characterises this as 'catalytic validity', arguing that it

> reorients, focuses, and energises participants toward knowing reality in order to transform it [.] (1986, p. 272)

The implications of this for research with and by oppressed groups are fairly clear. The constructions of such groups are commonly hidden by the hegemonic 'truths' of their oppressors, truths which are used to maintain existing inequalities and hence to perpetuate the oppressor–oppressed relationship. Seeking out the constructions of the oppressed, therefore, is not simply some exercise in curiosity, undertaken by the objective researcher of positivist methodology. Rather, it is a political act which critiques the constructions of the oppressors and makes possible emancipatory action which will transform the oppressive relationships of the groups involved.

In effect, as Lather implies, this redefinition of validity deflects attention away from *what* is said, and the correspondence between what is said and the 'real world', in order to refocus attention on *who* is speaking and their location in a nexus of oppressive social relations. Such a move constitutes a significant challenge for the professional intellectual. In so far as s/he speaks as a member of a privileged group, s/he may be unable to avoid articulating the hegemonic constructions of that group and thus unwittingly maintaining the oppression of the subjects of 'research'. Simply being who s/he is may disqualify her/him from valid utterance unless s/he unequivocally aligns him/herself with the oppressed.

On the other hand, the very fact that alternative definitions of 'validity' are possible at all is suggestive. Perhaps the stark choice between a discredited positivism and an unequivocal alignment with the oppressed is stark only in so far as one or other is seen as the pathway to some unequivocal truth. However, the availability of different definitions of validity opens up the possibility that we should think in terms, not of alternative pathways to 'the truth', but of pathways to *alternative* truths.

It is at this point that ideas derived from the work of Jürgen Habermas may be of help. Habermas (1986, 1987) argues that interactions between people are aimed at achieving an understanding on the basis of which further interaction can proceed. This they do by putting forward 'validity claims' of various kinds, which are effectively claims for the legitimacy of their points of view. Amongst these validity claims may be a claim to the *truthfulness* of a particular utterance. Habermas' primary concern, however, is not with establishing criteria for validity or truthfulness as such, but with exploring the sorts of claims which people actually make and with the different possible bases for such claims. His intention is thus not to find out what is 'true' about the world (in either a positivist or any other sense) but to determine the conditions under which people who understand the world differently can understand each other and engage in rational debate with each other.

Habermas' work is, it seems to me, particularly illuminating in relation to the positivist tradition in research and to the critiques of that tradition from a broadly emancipatory perspective. Two implications seem to follow from Habermas' analysis. First, the very different notions of validity in these approaches to research do not necessarily have to be seen as mutually exclusive. For all the adversarial positioning of emancipatory research *vis à vis* its positivist predecessor, it is possible for us to see them as simply making different sorts of claims to truthfulness. Put simply, positivist research is 'true' because it adheres to certain rules and procedures for accessing what is taken to be a 'real world'; emancipatory research is 'true' because it follows different rules and procedures to access the constructions of oppressed people. The 'truthfulness' of the one does not necessarily negate the 'truthfulness' of the other.

Second, Habermasian ideas may save us from a position of absolute relativity. The different forms of truthfulness which different forms of research claim are neither entirely arbitrary nor entirely unrelated to each other. Both positivist and emancipatory research make claims based on rule-bound and rigorous procedures. Within neither tradition is it possible to make capricious claims that something is the case; rather, procedures for establishing truthfulness have to be followed and these procedures have to be accepted by a group of peers. Moreover, although these procedures differ within the two traditions, they nonetheless can both be seen as falling within the domain of Habermasian truth-claims and can, in principle at least, be recognised as rule-bound and rigorous by researchers from different traditions. Potentially, therefore, there is the opportunity for dialogue *across* the two traditions which may be something more than adversarial confrontation.

It is, I suggest, this area of rational dialogue within which professional intellectuals can operate. Indeed, it seems to me that we already have examples of the sort of debate that I am advocating. A few commentators, for instance, have made explicit attempts to work across traditions in special needs research in order to find some way of relating their different approaches and findings to each other (Clark, Dyson and Millward, 1995; Skidmore, 1996; Stangvik, 1998). Similarly, Skrtic's (1995) recent attempt to offer an overview of thinking in this field, although firmly anti-positivist, seeks to embrace a range of alternative approaches and to find a way of allowing them to interact with each other. Perhaps even more significantly, the many serious-minded critiques of one tradition by the other can be read as rational engagements of precisely the sort I am advocating. *Making Difficulties* is, in fact, a case in point. Although the 'collective voice' of that volume is undoubtedly anti-positivist, its engagement with positivism is not mere posturing; on the contrary, it is an essentially *rational* interrogation of the truth-claims made within positivism and a *rational* advocacy of alternative claims. Moreover, one of the great strengths of *Making Difficulties* is that, because it contains accounts of researching as a career and a process, many of the contributors are able to illuminate the internal debates between different traditions which lie beneath the surface of their published work.

I wish to suggest, therefore, that there is a role for the professional intellectual as the instigator and sustainer of rational debate both within and between research traditions. Such a role requires neither a simplistic retreat into unreconstructed positivism, nor an unequivocal embrace of emancipatory principles. However, Habermas himself has frequently been criticised (Layder, 1994; Turner, 1988) for a naive faith in the possibility of rational debate undistorted by imbalances in power. It is important to be clear, therefore, that aligning the professional intellectual with the notion of rational debate is not the same as asserting that the intellectual is in some sense 'purely rational', or can enter that debate from a position which is above the interplay of interest and power. The role of the professional intellectual is one which emerges from a particular set of social relations and which undoubtedly represents and furthers the interests of particular social groups (Armstrong, Armstrong and Barton, 1998).

Moreover, there is no reason to suppose that the 'rational debate' as a whole is able to rise above the context of power and interest (Lather, 1990). Such debate is certainly open to the charge that rationality is frequently a cloak for oppression and that the careful consideration and balancing of options are luxuries which the powerful and comfortable can afford, but which the powerless and oppressed cannot. What I am arguing for, therefore, is not an absolute but a 'bounded' rationality (March and Simon, 1958). Such rationality consists not in reaching some position from which competing claims can be surveyed 'objectively', but in attempting to make claims explicit and to debate them according to rules which are consensual within a given community. Rationality in this sense is, of course, as subject to interrogation and critique as any of the claims which it seeks itself to interrogate. Furthermore, in the absence of any 'absolute' truth, the exercise of rationality does not place the professional intellectual above the necessity of making a commitment – explicit or otherwise – to values and stances through which that rationality is justified and which cannot, therefore, be themselves justified through rationality. The professional intellectual is thus committed to rationality *as a value* and, moreover, as a value which takes precedence over other values which might, for instance, lead to more direct action. For professional intellectuals who wish to see themselves as committed also to the interests of oppressed groups, the difference between this position and that of emancipatory researchers is slight, but significant. As I have argued above, emancipatory researchers seem to me also to be committed to rational debate. However, if I understand their position correctly, that commitment is justified in so far as rationality is placed *directly* in the service of oppressed groups. The professional intellectual, on the other hand, defers that direct dedication, interposing a commitment to the internal dynamics of rational debate between her/himself and the oppressed groups s/he wishes to believe that such a debate will ultimately benefit.

## A PROFESSIONAL INTELLECTUAL CRITIQUE OF 'VOICE'

I fully realise the extent to which the position I have just outlined is vulnerable both to manipulation in the interests of the already-powerful and to critique from an emancipatory position. I wish, therefore, to conclude this chapter by engaging in 'rational debate' with some of the key concepts in emancipatory research and in *Making Difficulties* itself. My aim is both to illustrate the sort of role which the professional intellectual can play, and to demonstrate, in so far as I am able, that such a role is not necessarily either conservative or oppressive.

A key theme in *Making Difficulties* and in a good deal of emancipatory research generally is one to which we have alluded in passing throughout this chapter, but which now deserves more serious scrutiny. That theme is formed by the interlinked notions of 'voice' (see, for instance, Barton and Clough's concluding chapter) and 'tale' or 'story' (see, for instance, Fulcher's chapter). I take these to be essentially postmodern concepts (Best and Kellner, 1991; Hassan, 1987) in that they arise from the notion that different individuals or groups construct their worlds in the way that storytellers construct their narratives. Hence, particular 'voices' tell those 'tales' which present the world as they wish or are constrained to see it. Given that many voices tell many, often conflicting, tales, the task of the researcher is thus to determine which 'voice' is to be taken note of and whose 'tale' is to be told. This task may seem simple when, as in the case of research in special educational needs and disability, the voices of an oppressed group have historically been silenced by other, more powerful groups. Indeed, in such cases, there may come a point where 'all' the researcher has to do is to stand to one side and enable members of that group to speak for themselves (see, for instance, Ballard, 1994).

However, as some of the uncertainties and questionings in *Making Difficulties* indicate, 'voice' and 'tale' are highly problematic concepts, even when applied to oppressed groups. In many cases, voices are far from clear and tales are far from coherent. Individuals, for instance, however oppressed, may not see themselves as belonging to particular groups; groups, even where they exist, may give rise to many contradictory voices; voices may tell many contradictory tales. Moreover, even at the individual level, it requires a peculiarly simplistic model of the individual to suppose that people necessarily speak with a single voice, or are able to give a coherent account of their lives and conditions, or have an unshakeable grasp on what lies in their best interests.

It follows that grounding the truth-claim of a piece of research on the notion of 'voice' involves making decisions about what constitutes the 'voice' of an individual, or which 'voice' within a group is representative of that group. If, moreover, voices are to be heard on the grounds that they speak for oppressed groups, then decisions are required about what constitutes oppression and which groups are, in fact, oppressed. Such decisions make it possible to foreground constructions of the social world which have previously gone unheard, and such foregrounding may well lead to illumination and open up possibilities for action. However, these decisions also close off possibilities: for every voice heard, another is silenced; for every group recognised as oppressed, another's oppression is denied or ignored.

Identifying decisions such as these enables us to delineate the nature of some of the truth-claims within emancipatory research. It does not in any sense demonstrate that such research is 'invalid' or 'untrue' – but it does tell us what sort of truth we are dealing with and therefore opens up spaces beyond that truth into which other sorts of truths can emerge. There is, I believe, a particularly illuminating example of this process in *Making Difficulties* in the form of Swain's reflexive and thoughtful account of his attempt to involve young people 'with special educational needs' in participatory research. In attempting to place himself as researcher at the disposal of these young people, Swain discovers that they are largely indifferent to the participatory role that is offered to them and construct the research process in ways which fail to coincide with his own construction. Unlike the participants in some versions of feminist research or disability research whose work Swain cites (Lather, 1986; Oliver, 1992a; Zarb, 1992), these young people apparently do not see themselves as belonging to an identifiable and oppressed group, and have no clearly defined political agenda which they wish to articulate. Moreover, their 'voices' and the 'tales' they tell are clearly embedded 'within the existing power relations and ideologies within the college' (p. 83) where they are enrolled. In other words, even when their voices are heard, they seem to betray a 'false consciousness' which is interposed between the accounts they give and what the researcher seems prepared to accept as the 'realities' within which they live.

If I understand Swain's analysis of this situation correctly, he is mainly concerned to account for the (relative) failure of his attempt to engage these young people in participatory research in terms of the distorting effects of power relations within the college. However, it seems to me that an alternative explanation is possible in terms of the boundaries of the emancipatory research paradigm itself. In so far as that paradigm seeks to foreground the voice of oppressed groups, it creates a very clear image of its 'subjects' – as oppressed, as constituting a group and as having a voice. This image is powerful in challenging the image created by positivist research of subjects who are passive, silent and reducible to their deficits and disabilities. Moreover, it is an image which matches well members of groups which are self-aware, politicised, articulate and bent on securing social change. Many disabled people might see themselves in such terms, as, indeed, would members of many other groups which have successfully participated in emancipatory research.

However, it is much less clear that this image is equally applicable to the group in Swain's research. These young people may well be oppressed, but there is little evidence that they *recognise* themselves as oppressed, nor that they have a coherent voice, nor that they are politicised, nor, indeed, that they see themselves as a coherent and distinct social group. Under these circumstances, research which proceeds on the basis of different assumptions may find it difficult to elicit a 'voice' which can be heard or to serve in any effective way the interests of these young people. Perhaps even more important, research which proceeds on the basis of assumptions about coherent voice and clear political agenda may foreground and advantage those groups who conform most clearly to that image at the expense of those groups which do not.

It is my contention that something of the sort is happening around the issues of disability and special educational needs currently. The powerful disability movement in the UK and beyond (Campbell and Oliver, 1996) has been extremely effective in foregrounding issues around disability and in challenging the images of disability informing both academic inquiry and policy-making. However, within education, issues around disability and issues around low attainment and disaffection have tended to be bundled together, not least since the creation of the 'super-category' of 'special educational needs' (Norwich, 1993). Whatever the advantages of such a move in stressing the commonalities between different groups, it also invites a contest between those groups and their advocates for control of the special educational needs policy agenda. It is at least arguable, for instance, that while one group seeks to deconstruct special educational needs in terms of a wider analysis of disability issues (Barton and Oliver, 1992; Oliver, 1988) and to reach out to other oppressed minorities (Corbett, 1996), another group seeks to deconstruct special educational needs in terms of a wider analysis of 'individual difference' and to reach out to the commonality of students (Ainscow, 1991, 1993, 1997; Booth, 1983; Dessent, 1987; Hart, 1996). Whilst good manners and a shared agenda normally maintains an alliance between these two groups, the occasional spat when they clash is illuminating (Oliver, 1992b).

In the light of this analysis, it may be more than merely coincidental that *Making Difficulties* claims in its subtitle to be about 'special educational needs' but then consistently elides special educational needs and disability as though they were one and the same thing. More significantly, some commentators have argued that particularly powerful arms of the disability movement tend to drive through policies which systematically disadvantage other groups (Fuchs and Fuchs, 1994), whilst Booth (1996; Booth, Ainscow and Dyson, 1997) has argued that the privileging of disability issues in the inclusion debate is serving to conceal the extent to which other groups are excluded from and within schools. Our analysis of Swain's chapter above, therefore, might be read as one more indication of how the very power and success of the disability movement may sometimes serve unwittingly to disadvantage other groups.

If this analysis is even partially correct, it raises important issues about the roles of emancipatory research and of the professional intellectual. The unconditional commitment to enabling the voices of oppressed groups to be heard which is at the heart of emancipatory research has, it seems to me, done much to problematise the easy assumptions of positivism and to expose the oppres-

sive impact of much – perhaps all – positivist research. A simple return to those
assumptions is, I would argue, out of the question and so too, therefore, is any
simple resumption of the role of the 'authoritative researcher voice'. Nonetheless, emancipatory research can itself be problematised. Its own founding assumptions and impacts are by no means unequivocally secure and benign. It is,
therefore, by no means clear that the power of its critique of positivist research
should lead us without reservation to reconstruct the role of the researcher
along emancipatory lines.

I return ultimately to Lather's notion of validity as arising in 'the generation
of counterpractices of authority' (1994, p. 40). If by 'authority' we mean the
hegemonic constructions of positivist researchers, then it is evident that the
critiques in *Making Difficulties* and beyond constitute precisely the sort of
counterpractices which are now needed. If, however, we mean by authority
*any* constructions which strive for hegemony, then it is equally evident that the
constructions of emancipatory research and its variants call for different sorts
of counterpractices in their own right. I contend that the promotion of rational
debate by professional intellectuals is one such counterpractice. It is, therefore,
as contributions to just such a debate that I welcome both *Making Difficulties*
and this new opportunity to respond to its critiques.


## REFERENCES

Ainscow, M. (1991) Effective schools for all: an alternative approach to special needs in
    education, in M. Ainscow (ed.) *Effective Schools for All*. London: David Fulton.
Ainscow, M. (1993) Towards effective schools for all: a reconsideration of the special
    needs task. Paper given in the seminar on Policy Options for Special Educational
    Needs in the 1990s, Institute of Education, University of London.
Ainscow, M. (1997) Towards inclusive schooling. *British Journal of Special Education*,
    Vol. 24, no. 1, pp. 3–6.
Armstrong, D., Armstrong, F. and Barton, L. (1998) From theory to practice: special
    education and the social relations of research production, in C. Clark, A. Dyson and
    A. Millward (eds.) *Theorising Special Education*. London: Routledge.
Ballard, K. (ed.) (1994) *Disability, Family, Whanau and Society*. Palmerston North,
    N.Z.: Dunmore Press.
Ballard, K. (1995) Inclusion, paradigms, power and participation, in C. Clark, A.
    Dyson and A. Millward (eds.) *Towards Inclusive Schools?* London: David Fulton.
Barnes, C. (1992) Qualitative research: valuable or irrelevant? *Disability, Handicap and
    Society (special issue)*, Vol. 7, no. 2, pp. 115–24.
Barton, L. (1994) Disability, difference and the politics of definition. *Australian Dis-
    ability Review*, Vol. 3, pp. 8–22.
Barton, L. and Clough, P. (1995) Conclusion: many urgent voices, in P. Clough and L.
    Barton (eds.) *Making Difficulties: Research and the Construction of Special Educa-
    tional Needs*. London: Paul Chapman.
Barton, L. and Oliver, M. (1992) Special needs: personal trouble or public issue? in M.
    Arnot and L. Barton (eds.) *Voicing Concerns: Sociological Perspectives on Contem-
    porary Education Reforms*. Wallingford: Triangle Books.

Best, S. and Kellner, D. (1991) *Postmodern Theory: Critical Interrogations*. New York: Guilford Press.

Bines, H. (1995) Risk, routine and reward: confronting the personal and social constructs in research on special educational needs, in P. Clough and L. Barton (eds.) *Making Difficulties: Research and the Construction of Special Educational Needs*. London: Paul Chapman Publishing.

Booth, T. (1983) Integration and participation in comprehensive schools. *Forum*, Vol. 25, no. 2, pp. 40–2.

Booth, T. (1996) A perspective on inclusion from England. *Cambridge Journal of Education*, Vol. 26, no. 1, pp. 87–99.

Booth, T., Ainscow, M. and Dyson, A. (1997) Understanding inclusion and exclusion in the English competitive education system. *International Journal of Inclusive Education*, Vol. 1, no. 4, pp. 337–54.

Campbell, J. and Oliver, M. (1996) *Disability Politics: Understanding our Past, Changing our Future*. London: Routledge.

Clark, C., Dyson, A. and Millward, A. (1995) Towards inclusive schools: mapping the field, in C. Clark, A. Dyson and A. Millward (eds.) *Towards Inclusive Schools?* London: David Fulton.

Clough, P. and Barton, L. (1995a) Introduction: self and the research act, in P. Clough and L. Barton (eds.) *Making Difficulties: Research and the Construction of Special Educational Needs*. London: Paul Chapman.

Clough, P. and Barton, L. (eds.) (1995b) *Making Difficulties: Research and the Construction of Special Educational Needs*. London: Paul Chapman.

Corbett, J. (1996) *Bad-Mouthing: the Language of Special Needs*. London: Falmer.

Dessent, T. (1987) *Making the Ordinary School Special*. London: Falmer.

Eisner, E. W. (1991) *The Enlightened Eye: Qualitative Inquiry and the Enhancement of Educational Practice*. New York: Macmillan.

Fuchs, D. and Fuchs, L. S. (1994) Inclusive schools movement and the radicalization of special education reform. *Exceptional Children*, Vol. 60, no. 4, pp. 294–309.

Fulcher, G. (1995) Excommunicating the severely disabled: struggles, policy and researching, in P. Clough and L. Barton (eds.) *Making Difficulties: Research and the Construction of Special Educational Needs*. London: Paul Chapman.

Gitlin, A., Bringhurst, K., Burns, M., Cooley, V., Myers, B., Price, K., Russell, R. and Tiess, P. (1992) *Teachers' Voices for School Change: An Introduction to Educative Research*. London: Routledge.

Guba, E. G. (1990a) The alternative paradigm dialog, in E. G. Guba (ed.) *The Paradigm Dialog*. London: Sage.

Guba, E. G. (ed.) (1990b) *The Paradigm Dialog*. London: Sage.

Habermas, J. (1986) *The Theory of Communicative Action, Volume I: Reason and the Rationalization of Society*. Cambridge: Polity Press.

Habermas, J. (1987) *The Theory of Communicative Action, Volume II: the Critique of Functionalist Reason*. Cambridge: Polity Press.

Hart, S. (1996) *Beyond Special Needs: Enhancing Children's Learning through Innovative Thinking*. London: Paul Chapman.

Hassan, I. (1987) *The Postmodern Turn: Essays in Postmodern Theory and Culture*: Columbus, Ohio State University Press.

Heron, J. (1988) Validity in co-operative inquiry, in P. Reason (ed.) *Human Inquiry in Action*. London: Sage.

Hill, J. (1995) Entering the unknown: case-study analysis in special schools, in P. Clough and L. Barton (eds.) *Making Difficulties: Research and the Construction of Special Educational Needs*. London: Paul Chapman.

Kincheloe, J. L. (1991) *Teachers as Researchers: Qualitative Inquiry as a Path to Empowerment*. London: Falmer.

Lather, P. (1986) Research as praxis. *Harvard Educational Review*, Vol. 56, no. 3, pp. 257–77.

Lather, P. (1990) Reinscribing otherwise: the play of values in the practices of the human sciences, in E. G. Guba (ed.) *The Paradigm Dialog*. London: Sage.

Lather, P. (1994) Fertile obsession: validity after poststructuralism, in A. Gitlin (ed.) *Power and Method: Political Activism and Educational Research*. London: Routledge.

Layder, D. (1994) *Understanding Social Theory*. London: Sage.

LeCompte, M. D. (1993) A framework for hearing silence: what does telling stories mean when we are supposed to be doing science?, in D. McLaughlin and W. G. Tierney (eds.) *Naming Silenced Lives: Personal Narratives and Processes of Educational Change*. London: Routledge.

Lincoln, Y. S. and Guba, E. G. (1985) *Naturalistic Inquiry*. Beverly Hills, Ca.: Sage.

March, J. and Simon, H. (1958) *Organizations*. New York: Wiley.

McLaughlin, D. and Tierney, W. G. (eds.) (1993) *Naming Silenced Lives: Personal Narratives and Processes of Educational Change*. London: Routledge.

Meekosha, H. and Jakubowicz, A. (1996) Disability, participation, representation and social justice, in C. Christensen and F. Rizvi (eds.) *Disability and the Dilemmas of Education and Justice*. Buckingham: Open University Press.

Norwich, B. (1993) Has 'special educational needs' outlived its usefulness? in J. Visser and G. Upton (eds.) *Special Education in Britain after Warnock*. London: David Fulton.

Oliver, M. (1988) The social and political context of educational policy: the case of special needs, in L. Barton (ed.) *The Politics of Special Educational Needs*. London: Falmer.

Oliver, M. (1992a) Changing the social relations of research production? *Disability, Handicap and Society*, Vol. 7, no. 2, pp. 101–14.

Oliver, M. (1992b) Intellectual masturbation: a rejoinder to Soder and Booth. *European Journal of Special Needs Education*, Vol. 7, no. 1, pp. 20–8.

Peters, S. (1995) Disability baggage: changing the education research terrain, in P. Clough and L. Barton (eds.) *Making Difficulties: Research and the Construction of Special Educational Needs*. London: Paul Chapman.

Reason, P. and Rowan, J. (eds.) (1981a) *Human Inquiry: a Sourcebook of New Paradigm Research*. Chichester: John Wiley.

Reason, P. and Rowan, J. (1981b) Issues of validity in new paradigm research, in P. Reason and J. Rowan (eds.) *Human Inquiry: a Sourcebook of New Paradigm Research*. Chichester: John Wiley.

Riddell, S., Brown, S. and Duffield, J. (1995) The ethics of policy-focused research in special educational needs, in P. Clough and L. Barton (eds.) *Making Difficulties: Research and the Construction of Special Educational Needs*. London: Paul Chapman.

Skidmore, D. (1996) Towards an integrated theoretical framework for research into special educational needs. *European Journal of Special Needs Education*, Vol. 11, no. 1, pp. 33–47.

Skrtic, T. M. (ed.) (1995) *Disability and Democracy: Reconstructing (Special) Education for Postmodernity*. New York: Teachers College Press.

Stangvik, G. (1998) Conflicting perspectives on learning disabilities, in C. Clark, A. Dyson and A. Millward (eds.) *Theorising Special Education*. London: Routledge.

Swain, J. (1995) Constructing participatory research: in principle and in practice, in P. Clough and L. Barton (eds.) *Making Difficulties: Research and the Construction of Special Educational Needs*. London: Paul Chapman.

Turner, J. (1988) *A Theory of Social Interaction*. Cambridge: Polity Press.

Vlachou, A. (1995) Images and the construction of identities in a research context, in P. Clough and L. Barton (eds.) *Making Difficulties: Research and the Construction of Special Educational Needs*. London: Paul Chapman.

Zarb, G. (1992) On the road to Damascus: first steps towards changing the relations of disability research production: *Disability, Handicap and Society (special issue)*, Vol. 7, no. 2, pp. 125–38.

# 2

# KNOWLEDGE IS NOT ENOUGH: AN EXPLORATION OF WHAT WE CAN EXPECT FROM ENQUIRIES WHICH ARE SOCIAL

## *Patricia Potts*

### INTRODUCTION

The research enquiries that I am involved in pursue questions about processes of inclusion in and exclusion from mainstream educational settings. I have studied the education systems of China and Hong Kong for some years now and am strengthening my links with colleagues in Spain and Sweden. As a result, the nature and possibilities of international comparative research are priority questions for me. A second main strand of my research work is the study of urban education, both here in the UK and in other countries. If processes of inclusion and exclusion are related to the capacity of educational services to provide appropriately for the full diversity of students, then the social, cultural and economic complexity of urban communities is bound to be a major locus of debate. A third strand of my work is the examination of power-relationships in education. This has led me to investigate a number of topics: the experience of women and girls, both today and over the past hundred years or so, the ways in which space and time are organised in educational settings and the ways in which stage-theories of child development and the language of assessment have sustained yardsticks of normality.

Alongside the content of questions about the aspects of education which interest me, my research activities entail asking further questions, about their form and their purposes. For me, the point of educational enquiry is to try and make sense of what is going on now. I also accept that I should take some responsibility for the consequences of these enquiries and, consequently, that developing policy and practice is a second fundamental aim. My research interests have grown out of my experience of school and university teaching and reflect my commitment to working towards a more democratic and inclusive system. The educational enquiries in which I participate are thus not neutral. They are themselves embedded in a network of social and political contexts.

In this chapter, I am going to explore the question of what kind of knowledge educational enquiries can expect to confirm. I shall discuss what is involved in making enquiries into processes of inclusion and exclusion and relate this to conditions for developing a critical approach. I shall conclude that defining educational enquiry as a quasi-physical or psychological science, in which social and political dimensions are avoided, marginalises the kind of knowledge which is most useful to teachers and learners. Moving towards an equitable system entails knowing less, not more.

## ENQUIRY AND RESPONSIBILITY

A starting-point for my discussion was the book *Making Difficulties* (Clough and Barton, 1995). In Chapter 1 the editors refer to the 'research act'. I like this. It sounds aggressive, dominating, gendered and makes you realise that there are important questions to ask about the justification for research. They argue that 'the framing, carrying out and reporting of research is an especially charged political act' (ibid., p. 147). Possible roles for researchers are discussed in the concluding section of the book: change agent, critical friend, someone who is accountable, a learner, a teacher, a subject; each one a value-laden social relationship.

However, given the self-aware and critical approach taken by the authors, what seems to me to be a contradiction leaps off the page. This is the use of the acronym 'SEN'. For it seems to me that 'special educational needs' is a phrase with no clear inherent meaning, but which functions to reinforce an enduring 'otherness'. Perhaps the very imprecision of the phrase is one reason why it is not criticised more frequently or systematically; its lack of grammar as a label and content as an identifier somehow soothing rather than unsettling? Or perhaps 'special educational needs' is seen as a more inclusive category than the former categories of 'handicap' and therefore less stigmatising?

Certainly, these issues don't matter very much to other writers. For example, in an article discussing values and rights in education, Geoff Lindsay states that one 'value position may be to ensure that all children with SEN receive education of a high standard, rather than that they should receive inclusive education' (Lindsay, 1997, p. 57). Here, the grammar of 'SEN' operates just as if it were an old-style category of handicap, an attribute of those for whom it is has also become the identifying label. This enables Geoff Lindsay to separate, even place in opposition, 'high standard' education from the ethical issues which are explored in *Making Difficulties*.

Geoff Lindsay argues that 'terms' could never be as important as the 'existence' of a group of people (Lindsay, 1997, p. 56), thus trivialising the ine-

qualities of identity, voice and power that characterise many research activities. This position leads him to write, not only in contradiction of what he
has said about educational standards but also in contradiction of what he has
said about the comparative irrelevance of the issue of rights. 'Implicit (in
education) is valuing the child with SEN as having the same rights as other
children and requiring society collectively to help that child' (ibid., p. 56).
Using the language of 'SEN' seems to have drained the current writer of his
critical awareness and diminished his responsibility as a self-reflective teacher
and researcher towards the dissemination of official and professional rhetoric.

## VARIETIES OF KNOWING

Once upon a time I was a student of philosophy. We debated what might be
the necessary and sufficient conditions for asserting the truth of a statement
and we asked what might be the relationship between true statements and
knowing. We discovered that there are different kinds of true statement and
different kinds of knowing. We also discovered that it is possible to know
things which do not satisfy certain conditions for the establishment of truth.
Our discussions branched out in several directions: into the structure of scientific explanations and into the distinction between knowledge and belief. The
first topic raised questions about the relationship between evidence and argument in situations which could be expected to produce law-like conclusions;
the second raised questions about the possibility of knowing in situations
which were not accessible to concrete demonstration. We then went on to
study the arguments of rationalists and empiricists about the relationship between different methods of enquiry and the relative epistemological status of
their conclusions. Lastly, we observed that, despite the logical mistake of
assuming an 'ought' from an 'is', it is impossible to separate facts and values.
    These discussions have informed my experience of and thinking about enqu-
iries into the social practice of education. I do not expect to communicate
research findings by means of generalisably true statements. I do expect to
work towards contingently true statements. This distinction, between generalisable and contingent truth, is one which Lawrence Stenhouse illustrated by
contrasting what he describes as 'scientific' and 'historical' narratives:

> History . . . is the expression of a systematic critical enquiry into the fruits of our
> experience . . . Science aspires to generalisations which are predictive and univer-
> sal, whereas historical generalisation is retrospective and summarises experience
> within boundaries of time and place . . . (History) enables us to make judgemental
> predictions of how events will go and to revise those predictions in the face of
> surprise by rapid reassessments . . . When we apply science we premise high
> predictability and when we apply history we premise low predictability. I believe
> that the acts and thoughts of individual human beings contain essentially unpre-
> dictable elements owing to the human capacity for creative problem-solving and

the creation of meanings. Others, of course, will see unpredictability in human action as the wilderness beyond the advancing frontier of a social science. (Stenhouse, 1981, p. 106).

## KNOWLEDGE AND TRUTH

My experience of supervising postgraduate students indicates that, while many of them perceive the irrelevance of a scientific paradigm to their particular projects, instead of developing a confident critique, they feel obliged to apologise. The task of supporting their progress towards an autonomous critical voice has turned out to be as much about raising their consciousness of themselves as about matching their research questions to relevant methods of enquiry and analysis. It seems to me that there is a direct link between increasing their participation in their own learning and developing their capacity for critical analysis. The corollary is clear: that, without a sense of identity and self-worth, people find it difficult to engage with this sort of task. What is the case for inexperienced researchers is also the case for their teachers and supervisers.

In the positivist paradigm, the aim is to be able to control and therefore predict the behaviour of those features of the world that are under scrutiny. The assumption of fact is that a conclusion can be reached whose truth-value is certain and immutable. The assumption of value is that this is the best form of scientific enquiry.

The reassurance and potential simplicity of this approach is so attractive that the paradigm is imposed upon many features of the world whose significance may not be accessible to this form of enquiry. This is not surprising, given that scientific methods of enquiry are seen as the way to render the world intelligible. But it leads to the kind of inconsistency that we see when students are taught about the value of small-group work and discussion in the context of a whole-class, non-participatory lecture. For example, an enquiry that asks questions about the possibilities of re-admitting to the educational mainstream students who have been excluded but which does not ask questions about the process of classification by which the students have been identified as ineligible, implies that the study of inclusion can be undertaken sensibly within a methodology which assumes that categorical labels are the result of a satisfactory analysis of people's lives.

A social category like 'emotionally and behaviourally disturbed', as well as purporting to describe those contained within its boundaries, functions to confirm a polarised, 'not like us', value-judgement. Biologist Steven Rose describes enquiries which rely on this sort of classification as robotic, a denial of personal and social agency. He gives an example of the irresponsible way in which irrelevant categories of fearful otherness can be constructed and manipulated:

> There is embedded within the ideological reductionist paradigm a cascade of conceptual errors. These begin with arbitrary agglomeration – lumping together many different phenomena as if they are all exemplars of the same underlying

process. Next comes reification – turning complex social processes involving several participating individuals into 'things' or 'tendencies' located in the biology of individual participants. Inappropriate quantification assumes that such 'lumps' can be measured, so that it becomes possible to say of one individual that they are twice as aggressive as another, or to rank the entire population along a linear scale of 'intelligence' measured by IQ tests . . . Finally, there comes what I describe as evolutionary fantasies . . . 'Aggression' provides a good example. A standard technique in quantifying such behaviour is to find an 'animal model', in this case rats, which when placed in a confined tank and presented with mice, will often kill them. How fast a rat kills a mouse, and the hormonal and brain processes that trigger such mouse-killing, are taken as surrogates in explaining the causes of drive-by shootings among Los Angeles gangs. (Rose, 1997, pp. 16–17).

Another reason for the denial of the social nature of research is the perceived need for objectivity. This implies that what or who is studied is passive and that enquirers can and should undertake analyses from the perspective of a reality that does not interact with that inhabited by the objects of their studies. The kind of true statements that might result from such an approach are assumed to have a purity and independence that can be trusted. In an article discussing research into disability and inclusive education, Keith Ballard rejects this scientific distance:

> A key issue both in a move from positivism and the call for researcher engagement with the lived experience of disabled people is that of researcher participation with those they would learn with and from. Reducing the distance between researcher and researched . . . parallels, and is related to, the issue of disabilism in society in general, in which disability is created as distant and unfamiliar. Those we do not know we construct as 'other' than ourselves. Researchers who are not themselves disabled may reflect their community's lack of experience and understanding of disability. Their construction of the disabled as 'other' will have implications for their research and for themselves. (Ballard, 1997, p. 246)

Keith Ballard outlines a methodology which recognises the moral and political dimensions of social research. He makes the link between reducing the distance between enquirer and research participants and reducing the distance between disabled and non-disabled people in educational services. Fear of the unknown generates a need to isolate and control its source. Direct experience can overcome the fear and, consequently, the need to control. With the dissolution of the category of 'other', the rationale for the segregation of disabled students from the educational mainstream loses its force.


## AUTHORITY

I have described a positivist ideal whose charisma may well be fading, not only in social research methodologies but also in the physical sciences themselves. However, the caricature serves to illustrate a set of connections between truth and knowledge which still resonate and which surface in a range of pedagogical contexts. For example, students following a research degree programme for education practitioners received advice from tutors on a separate, but prerequisite, methodology course not to consider the preparation of case studies of pupils or settings that they are familiar with because this would constitute 'researcher-bias'. Again, I have a friend and colleague, a senior local education authority officer, who, when making enquiries about registering for a research degree, which she imagined would be based on her key role in educational policy and practice in several different areas over the last fifteen years, was told that she should first attend a course for inexperienced researchers, after which she would be encouraged to undertake a research project in areas of the UK of which she knew nothing. What sense can be made of advice given to experienced people to forget what they have learned in practice and thus sever the links between their enquiries and the origins of their research questions?

Keith Ballard reminds us that the aim of objective distance is as much about social relations as it is about epistemology. To learn or not to learn from experience? This is a question whose answers are political. An approach to making enquiries in which participating researchers are encouraged to begin by excluding themselves controls not only the subject-matter of any investigation but also the legitimacy of their voice. Colin Barnes has described this process as the construction of a 'myth':

> If disability research is about researching oppression and I would argue that it is, then researchers should not be professing 'mythical independence' to disabled people but joining them in their struggles to confront and overcome this oppression. Researchers should be espousing commitment, not value freedom, engagement not objectivity and solidarity not independence. (Barnes, 1996, p. 110)

As in 'research', so in life. A PhD student I am working with is embarking on a study of the learning experiences of young men and women in a college of further education. She has written about an incident at the college in which the young people's course choices and timetables, the result of many hours of collaborative work, were thrown out in twenty minutes by senior managers. What could have caused this contradiction of the college's explicit values of autonomy and respect, in which the lecturers as well as the students were publicly devalued? Our research student is trying to understand events in terms of the perspective of all concerned, including managers, who, she has discovered, were under a great deal of pressure, especially over funding. However, these concerns were not shared and their decisions therefore came as a shock. The managers looked at 'statistics and resourcing'; students were seen as 'numbers or units of funding' (Owen, 1997). The distance of the managers from the students seems to have enabled them to deny that the situation was both complex and social. Maintaining control over the institution is thus associated with a hierarchical, non-participatory structure.

Listening to the voices of all groups involved would have meant letting go of control and recognising that the desire for simple, completed, discrete action is illegitimate. As in life, so in systematic social enquiry. Listening to the voices of everyone involved leads to transformations (unpredictable, never-ending) both of social relationships and of approaches to social enquiry. As Lawrence Stenhouse indicated, this will be welcome to some people and anathema to others.

When the degradation of residents in long-stay hospitals was exposed nearly twenty years ago, the inhumanity of their living conditions was understood to be related to their invisibility and their silence (see Oswin, 1978; Ryan and Thomas, 1981; Shearer, 1981). The distance between people then classified as 'mentally handicapped' and people classified as 'professionals' or 'normal' had been too great to support any two-way communication. Telling the stories of these forgotten people in their own words and imagery has therefore become a social, political and epistemological imperative.

Dorothy Atkinson supports people who experience difficulties in communication to prepare their own versions of their life histories and she describes her approach as auto/biographical:

> Auto/biographical research can have an impact at both a personal and a social level. At a personal level, it provides the opportunity for people with learning disabilities to look at and make sense of their own lives. In enabling people to compile their autobiographies, it involves them in the process of life review.
>
> At a social level, the collecting of auto/biographical accounts can bring out the commonalities as well as the differences in people's experiences – commonalities with other people with learning disabilities, as well as with the rest of society. This has the potential to encourage social and historical awareness and understanding, of shared experiences and their sources, for people with learning disabilities. And, just as importantly, auto/biographical research provides a means by which the understanding of others can be enriched – so we can begin to know what it means and what it has meant, to be seen as a person with a learning disability in this society. (Atkinson, 1997, p. 2)

Taking an auto/biographical approach to making sense of social experience involves the interpretation, not only of the perspectives of those about whose lives questions are asked but also of the perspectives of those who ask the questions. Dorothy Atkinson writes about her research in the first person: 'there is my voice too, for in working with people, transcribing their words and assembling a collective account, this is also my story' (Atkinson, 1997, p. 22). The recognition of the inevitably autobiographical character of my own writing both simplifies and complicates: it is a release to value my own perspectives but their explicit inclusion adds layers to the already intricate work of analysis.

For Dorothy Atkinson writing in the first person is integral to the development of critical reflection. For example, she realised that there were rhythms to any project that cannot be controlled in advance:

> What I would do differently now would be to negotiate joint aims with research participants, rather than attempt to impose my own . . .
>
> The other thing that I would do differently now is to think about time more realistically. I had originally assumed that I could do some quick research, simply

testing a method over a few weeks. This was unrealistic, but so, too, for many people, would be the two years that I eventually spent. . . . We needed time, as all groups do, to develop trust and commitment, but we also needed time to sort out our conflicting agendas. This took a long time. . . . The sense of togetherness which then prevailed, however, meant that the group developed a life and momentum of its own. And this took more time . . .

Initially it was my wish that we should work together on co-constructing history. That wish later came to be shared, but it took a long time. There was a prior need, it seemed, for individual group members to make sense of their own lives first before seeing these lives in a wider context. The historical account is not, therefore, as strong as it might have been had we worked on it together from an earlier stage. (Atkinson, 1997, pp. 127, 128 and 130)

An auto/biographical approach to social enquiry is useful, then, not because its conclusions are generalisable. Quite the reverse. Apart from making a positive difference to the lives of participants, it enables enquirers to develop an understanding whose worth is directly related to its transience. Valuable social knowledge is bound to change, as those who want to know, those who contribute to the knowing and the contexts in which questions are asked also change.

## INDIVIDUALISM

Strong arguments are, however, put forward for the rejection of an auto/biographical approach to social research. For example, that the promotion of such a methodology lays people without power open to abuse because the publication of the stories of those whose lives have not carried weight in the past can be used by whoever has access to them in whatever way they want. Those who support this position argue that a more effective way to redress social inequalities is to concentrate on the collection of information from large numbers of people which can be presented in formats which have greater impact.

Counter-arguments include that the process of 'speaking-up' is, itself, empowering and that the risk of abuse is no greater than with any other approach, though the risk of personal hurt may be higher. Even then, this may be no reason not to validate people's lives through the construction of their autobiography. If there is abuse of these histories then this should trigger a public and constructive response. Further, an auto/biographical approach implies a reciprocity, whereby people of differing social status acknowledge their personal perspectives and interests.

Another argument against taking an individualised approach is that it will be associated with theoretical positions which take people out of their cultural, economic and political contexts and interpret their lives in terms of universal typologies or worse, pathologies. This depoliticised approach can result in the sort of victimisation in which individuals are seen both as deficient and as responsible for the difficulties they experience. The medical model of disability is one example of the denial of the social construction of barriers to living and learning.

Reviewing a book on the sexual politics of disability, Mike Oliver expresses this argument in the following terms:

> The social model, as I understand it, refuses to abstract individuals from their society and history, and sees empowerment as an essentially collective phenomenon. (Oliver, 1998)

Colin Barnes agrees, criticising the 'true confessions brigade, those intent on writing about themselves rather than engaging in serious political analysis of a society that is inherently disabling for increasingly large sections of the population' (Barnes, 1998).

My counter-argument, here, would be that respect for the lives of particular individuals, whom we know by name, is quite different from the approach which sees individuals as nameless representatives of social types. I would also argue that the denial of the effects of personal experience weakens, rather than strengthens, the power of relevant theoretical understandings.

In an article about undertaking what they call 'narrative' research with people who experience difficulties in communication, Tim and Wendy Booth defend the attention they have paid to one young man:

> There is another reason too for paying attention to Danny Avebury. Too often the problems of interviewing inarticulate subjects are seen in term of their deficits rather than the limitations of our methods. Such a 'deficit model' of informant response is rooted in a view of disability as a problem of the individual. It serves to legitimate the exclusion of, for example, people with learning difficulties from a participatory role in narrative research in ways that mirror their exclusion from the wider society. The emphasis of research should be on overcoming the barriers that impede the involvement of inarticulate subjects instead of highlighting the difficulties they represent . . .
>
> It is too easy as a narrative researcher not to bother with people like Danny. . . . There is a danger of allowing ourselves to be drawn by the tempo of our times into a kind of 'fast research' with a premium on quick results. Against this background, it is important to remember the virtues of an older, anthropological tradition which recognised that the task of learning to communicate with subjects takes a long time. Narrative researchers must go back to such basics in order to ensure that their scholarship does not continue to silence the stories of people like Danny Avebury. (Booth and Booth, 1996, p. 67)

I think that there are ambiguities in the way we use the terms 'individualism' and 'individualistic'. The individualism which arises from an interest in responding to diversity is not the same as the individualism which arises from an interest in fixed mental deficits.

## ASKING QUESTIONS ABOUT PROCESSES OF INCLUSION AND EXCLUSION

All arguments begin with an assumption, which often takes the form of a definition. As I have already indicated, we should expect this to be both a description of fact and a judgement of value. My own research focuses on the overcoming of barriers to learning and my experience of education systems leads me to assume first, that barriers arise when curricula are not responsive to the perspectives and requirements of students and second, that barriers arise in social contexts and are therefore variable. Further, my experience leads me to assume that increasing the participation of all students within mainstream educational settings will contribute to the reduction of their difficulties in learning because I make a link between this process of inclusion and the implementation of policies directed at reducing inequalities arising from students' culture, race, gender, disability or level of attainment. Consequently, my enquiries should be directed towards an examination of these assumptions.

Criteria for evaluating moves towards or away from inclusion in educational settings are bound to reflect the way in which inclusion has been defined. The clearer the definition, from whatever perspective it has been derived, the greater the possibility for critical analysis. A range of criteria follows from the definition that I have assumed. For example, access to curricular and extra-curricular activities, flexible forms of assessment and reducing exclusion at secondary transfer; equality of opportunity for members of staff, integrated support services and combined professional development; parental participation. These areas constitute one possible framework, constructed in a particular place and time, for examining assumptions about the effects of increasing student participation, about the variability of their experiences of difficulty and about the link between membership of the mainstream and reducing inequalities.

However, Chris Woodhead, Chief Inspector of Schools in England and Wales, has outlined support for an approach to educational research which is asocial and apolitical. He has been reported as saying that he 'wants academics to study the effectiveness of teaching methods rather than try to identify gender, class or race bias' (O'Reilly and Barot, 1997). This is a broadside against the work of many practising researchers, including those of us for whom the identifying and overcoming of barriers to learning are specific responsibilities. I began to wonder if the Chief Inspector's view is not as socially and politically embedded as those whose work he attacks.

The current focus on the effectiveness of schools can be traced back to the publication of *Fifteen Thousand Hours*, the study carried out in secondary schools in the 1970s under the direction of psychiatrist Michael Rutter. This research demonstrated that there were many ways in which schools made a difference to the attainments of their students and, in doing so, reacted against the view that the influence of social and economic factors obliterated anything that that schools themselves might be able to achieve. The legacy of this study has been a swing away from the contexts of schooling towards the examination of classroom and staffroom life. Has it been forgotten, though, that the project's analysis of school processes did not include any direct investigation of curricula or teaching? As the authors said: 'We did not attempt to study the curriculum or the content of classroom teaching as such' (Rutter *et al.*, 1979, p. 107).

There are some implications that seem to me to be relevant to draw out here. Firstly, while *Fifteen Thousand Hours* may have been valuable in raising awareness of how significant is the ethos of a school as an influence on the attainment levels of its students, it also set a climate in which the social experience of teaching and learning could be neglected in favour of an operational definition of 'ethos' which was compatible with a view of educational research as technology and in which the question 'effective for what?' could be left unasked.

Secondly, while this approach implicitly recognised that the social relationships of teaching and learning are too complex to be filtered through a matrix of quantitative measurements, it nevertheless clung to the conception of educational enquiry as a scientific discipline, modelled on clinical psychology, rather than attempting to respond with a more appropriate methodology to what the researchers knew about the characteristics of schooling. Adherence to a technical view of educational research, in which questions about the social contexts of teaching and learning are outlawed, is not itself a value-free position.

## A RATIONAL APPROACH

One recent contribution to making sense of the experiences of children about whose learning their teachers are concerned is Susan Hart's book *Beyond Special Needs* (Hart, 1996). Her approach is strikingly rationalist, encouraging teachers to extend their understanding of their pupils' perspectives by means of a conscious dialectic, a sequence of questions which aim to utilise knowledge, perceptions and ideas which might otherwise have lain dormant. Her close study of individual children has led Susan Hart to argue that acceptance, attention and respect are the foundation for overcoming barriers to learning. She calls this the acknowledgement of students. Her moral commitment to the human rights of the young children she writes about is as much a part of her approach as her disciplined analysis of their conversations and work. Although I have criticised this book for appearing to respond more warmly to Adrian than to Annette, an unintended bias which I see as one of the problems of her approach, I agree that a resolution to acknowledge students would make a profound difference to their experiences of learning.

I have discussed my interpretation with Susan Hart. She said, if I accepted her argument that there will always be aspects of a situation that go unexamined, then I should have expected her account to be incomplete. She also responded by saying that her approach does not imply that gender, for example, is not important, only that, here, she chose not to bring it in as a dimension of analysis. I wondered about this and argued that, in omitting an explicit discussion of gender, it may seem to have been devalued as a relevant factor. Could her systematic analysis of individual experiences of learning have been combined with a consideration of its contexts that went some way to reflect the complexities involved, without rendering the narrative too unwieldy or incoherent?

Susan Hart's book has definitely illuminated my thinking. However, it would not be accurate to say that I was not already aware of the main tenets of her thesis nor that my agreement stems from knowledge I have gained solely from sources identifying themselves as educational research. Do we know, at least for here and now, that people flourish in circumstances of acceptance, attention and respect or do we not? If so, are we allowing social research which ignores it to make us stupid?

## CONCLUSION

I began by outlining the research projects I am involved with and discussing the relationship, firstly between the questions that interest me and the form that my enquiries should take and secondly, between my enquiries and their social consequences. I then asked what kind of knowledge educational enquiries could hope to confirm and what kind of knowledge would be useful to learners and teachers. It seemed to me that what can be learned from educational enquiries is neither generalisable nor objective and that multi-faceted inter-pretations are much more useful, as they acknowledge inescapable social and political complexities.

Recognising that inequalities of power exist in 'research' as in life has led some enquirers to share control of projects with participants and actively work towards the strengthening of their voices. Autobiographical approaches to social research have been criticised, however, for laying participants open to subsequent abuse thus perpetuating rather than reducing powerlessness. For these critics, the authenticity of individual 'voices' cannot be as effective in securing political change as a social theory based on collective experience.

I gave some examples of inconsistency and confusion over the relationship between language, rights and educational practice and I also gave an example of an approach to educational research that I find impressive and empowering.

I have argued that the kind of research I am involved with is at odds with that which is currently sanctioned by the government because of the explicit discouragement of investigations into social inequalities. I have also argued that what is presented as a value-free approach is as socially and politically embedded as any other.

I have outlined what I see as a deep-rooted problem for educational enquiry, which stems from my discussion of what kind of knowledge can be expected to follow from social research and from an awareness that facts and values are inseparable. If an equitable society is an agreed goal, then classification systems will be undermined. If the achievement of certain knowledge is valued, then classification systems will be shored up. These scenarios are incompatible. There is tension between an epistemological need to tighten-up definitions and an ethical need to loosen them. How much unintelligibility can we tolerate for the sake of equity? How much categorising can we tolerate for the sake of knowledge? I think of this situation as a 'democratic dilemma'.

I conclude that certain knowledge could not be enough to answer my questions about processes of inclusion in and exclusion from education. Only knowledge that can reflect the political and cognitive instabilities of increasing equality could be really useful.

## REFERENCES

Atkinson, D. (1997) *An Auto/biographical Approach to Learning Disability Research.* Aldershot: Ashgate.

Ballard, K. (1997) Researching disability and inclusive education: participation, construction and interpretation. *International Journal of Inclusive Education,* Vol. 1, no. 3, pp. 243–56.

Barnes, C. (1996) Disability and the myth of the independent researcher, *Disability and Society,* Vol. 11, no. 1 pp. 107–10.

Barnes, C. (1998) Review of *The Rejected Body: Feminist Philosophical Reflections on Disability,* by Susan Wendell (1996), London: Routledge. *Disability and Society,* Vol. 13, no. 1, pp. 145–6.

Booth, T. and Booth, W. (1996) Sounds of silence: narrative research with inarticulate subjects. *Disability and Society,* Vol. 11, no. 1, pp. 55–70.

Clough, P. and Barton, L. (eds.) (1995) *Making Difficulties. Research and the Construction of Special Educational Needs.* London: Paul Chapman.

Hart, S. (1996) *Beyond Special Needs: Enhancing Children's Learning Through Innovative Thinking.* London: Paul Chapman.

Lindsay, G. (1997) Values, rights and dilemmas. *British Journal of Special Education,* Vol. 24, no. 2, pp. 55–9.

Oliver, M. (1998) Review of *The Sexual Politics of Disability: Untold Desires,* by Tom Shakespeare, Kath Gillespie-Sells and Dominic Davies (1997), London: Cassell. *Disability and Society,* Vol. 13, no. 1, pp. 150–2.

O'Reilly and Barot (1997) Woodhead in purge of PC school research. *Sunday Times,* 31 August, p. 7.

Oswin, M. (1978) *Children Living in Long Stay Hospitals.* London: Spastics International Medical Publications/Heinemann.

Owen, S. (1997) Further education and students in transition: issues arising from pre-literature-study observations. Unpublished research assignment.

Rose, S. (1997) When making things simple does not give the right explanation. *Times Educational Supplement,* 5 September, pp. 16–17.

Rutter, M., Maughan, B., Mortimore, P. and Ouston, J. (1979) *Fifteen Thousand Hours: Secondary Schools and their Effects on Children.* London: Open Books.

Ryan, J. and Thomas, F. (1981) *The Politics of Mental Handicap.* Harmondsworth: Penguin.

Shearer, A. (1981) *Disability: Whose Handicap?* Oxford: Blackwell.

Stenhouse, L. (1981) What counts as research? *British Journal of Educational Studies,* Vol. 29, no. 2, pp. 103–14.

# 3

# DEVELOPING AN EMANCIPATORY RESEARCH AGENDA: POSSIBILITIES AND DILEMMAS

## *Len Barton*

### INTRODUCTION

In the previous edited collection of papers (Clough and Barton, 1995) and in this volume a strong emphasis of research as a social act is clearly articulated. Such an approach raises questions about the relationship between participants in a research project, the ethics involved and the complex interplay between biography, situation and wider socio-economic conditions and relations within which the research takes place. The sociality of the research process entails the art of listening to a variety of voices and through interaction with others developing a greater self-understanding that is the outcome of a critical stance towards one's own presuppositions, priorities and practices. Understanding self and others in this way is one of the essential preconditions of change and is thus a crucial element in seeking to re-examine the question of what constitutes effective, enabling research.

### A QUESTION OF VOICE

It is essential when considering the question of 'voice' in relation to educational research that we are aware of, and seek to learn from, the struggles disabled people have been and still are involved in outside the educational context. Thus, engagement with the issue of 'voice' has a history in disability politics. For example, Connelly (1990) maintains, that in relation to social service departments disabled people have been struggling to have:

- a voice in relation to their own circumstances;

- to have a voice in reacting to services currently used or contributing to the design or management of services;

- to have an input into the work of the department through participation in training, in planning or advisory groups of various kinds, or as staff or councillors. (p. 3)

This demand is based on the historical understanding that disabled people as individuals or organisations have been excluded from such possibilities. 'Voice' thus implies participating in decision-making that will have a real impact on their lives.

Connelly also alerts us to the various structural, institutional and attitudinal barriers to participation including the impact of learned helplessness and socialisation into a dependency role; a sense of failure arising from lack of support and success in previous attempts at independence; and little awareness of the extent of choice available over a range of aspects of their everyday lives.

It is against this disabling context that the notion of 'voice' is to be understood. It is part of the struggle for self and collective pride on the part of disabled people. This includes expressing choices and decisions on matters affecting their lives. For Connelly (1990, p. 24) this gives rise to several significant questions including: What opportunities are there for expressing such voices? Do the opportunities ensure that these voices are listened to? Does change occur? Whilst these questions are directed towards social services departments and practices, they are equally applicable to the issue of educational research.

## THE STRUGGLE FOR AN ALTERNATIVE APPROACH

Research is a demanding activity involving complex relationships and negotiations and decision-making and is often experienced as an essentially private practice. Questions concerning why, how and with what consequences specific decisions are made at particular points in a research project are often taken for granted and thus remain unexamined. In an attempt to make the research act more visible, to demystify the process through self-disclosure and critical reflection, more researchers are endeavouring to share their insights and experiences (Barnes and Mercer, 1998; Moore, Beazley and Maelzer, 1998; Connelly and Troyna, 1998). This volume is to be seen as contributing to these approaches.

This revelationary activity entails the identification and exploration of difficult and fundamental questions including: Why is the topic of research important? How were the topic and the research questions arrived at? What is (are) the purpose(s) of the research? For whose benefit is the research undertaken? Who owns the data? Whilst such questions are applicable to research generally, they have a particular significance when considered in relation to excluded and oppressed groups.

Engaging with these questions is not a minor task in that it is about challenging power-relations, cultures of dependency and a range of disabling practices. It concerns the issue of control, the nature of participation and the ethics of the research process. This is not a smooth, linear process. It is disturbing, complicated, contradictory and extremely demanding on time, thought and emotions. For the researcher, recognising oneself as a learner, cultivating a sense of humility in the light of the richness and profundity of the human subject and one's own limited skills and understandings, appreciating that one's work is never final or beyond criticism and thus always partial and incomplete, are crucial elements of the critical self-awareness that is being advocated.

Research is not merely about developing more sophisticated skills of, for example, observation and technical abilities. It is crucially about *relationships* and involves establishing and maintaining powers of definition and decision-making between the different participants. How key concepts are defined within a project, whose interests such definitions serve, are questions that a self-critical stance towards research is interested in.

## LOOKING BACK – LOOKING FORWARD

In one of the most seminal papers on disability research, Oliver (1992), a disabled scholar, contends that research has become part of the disabling barriers within society in that too often it has been undertaken in ways that have been alienating. In a most forceful manner he maintains that for disabled people research has been:

> a violation of their experience, as irrelevant to their needs and as failing to improve their material circumstances and quality of life. (p. 105)

Such research has contributed to the development and maintenance of an individualised model of disability in which the problems are located within the person.

The fundamental point which Oliver carefully presents is that such failings are attributable to the social relations of research production. He argues that:

> The social relations of research production provides the structure within which research is undertaken. These social relations are built upon a firm distinction between the researchers and researched; upon the belief that it is the researchers who have specialist knowledge and skills; and that it is they who decide what topics should be researched and be in control of the whole process of research production. (p. 102)

It is important to be clear as to what Oliver is arguing for. He is not advocating that research has nothing to contribute to the well-being of society or particular groups. Nor is he maintaining that only disabled researchers should be involved in research. What he is seeking to encourage is a fundamental shift in the ways in which we think about research, including the purpose, process and outcomes of these activities. He wants to see the introduction of a 'different set of social relations of research production' which will provide the possibility for a more enabling, or what he terms 'emancipatory', form of research activity.

The issue of educational research has come under severe criticism both from within the research community and from a range of internal and external sources including the Chief Inspector of Schools, journalists and other new right ideologues (Hargreaves, 1996a, 1996b; O'Reilly and Barot, 1997; Smithers, 1995). Whilst representing a range of perspectives there are some common features of these critiques, including: the waste of limited financial resources; the jargon-ridden nature of the work; the political bias of much of the material; and finally, the lack of relevance to schools and classrooms.

In an article about the test of research quality, Smithers (1995) contends that:

> If the criterion of *usefulness* were adopted, we should have some reasonable hope of creating a field of inquiry valued by those it is intended to serve.

A superficial reading of such criticism and those articulated by disabled people could be used to maintain a link between these perspectives. However, this would be to miss some fundamental differences between the approaches. Disabled scholars and organisations of disabled people are arguing for a relevance that is, firstly, explicitly concerned with issues of social justice, equity and citizenship which inevitably necessitates addressing political issues and is not to be viewed as disinterested or neutral research. Secondly, relevant research in this field needs to be concerned with the struggle for change and thus a critical engagement with, for example, material and ideological barriers to participation. This form of relevant research is not about tips for living, but about institutional discrimination, exclusion and the lack of political will at a local and central state level to engage with these issues. Finally, relevant research is essentially transformative, contributing information to the collective experience and understanding of disabled people over the ways in which disability is socially produced (Oliver, 1997; Shakespeare and Watson, 1997; Barnes, 1996; Morris, 1992; and Abberley, 1992).

What is being encouraged is a form of research in which disabled people are empowered. This is not, as Oliver argues, 'a gift of the few who have it to be delivered to those who do not' (p. 11). It is about people empowering themselves and using the knowledge and the 'expertise' of the researcher towards this end. It will have serious methodological changes if, as he argues, there needs to be the establishment and maintenance of 'trust and respect and participation and reciprocity' (p. 106) between both parties.

The vision which Oliver is presenting is one of a research activity that is transformative, relevant to and significant in the lives of disabled people. This he believes is part of the struggle against oppression and in which he asks researchers to join disabled people and use their expertise and skills in a common cause (p. 102). For those of us who are ultimately concerned with the realisation of an inclusive society such an issue goes well beyond disablement and is applicable to researchers working with all forms of marginalised and oppressed groups (Barnes, 1991).


## INSIDER ACCOUNTS

In a refreshingly open, readable and highly reflective account of research practices, Moore, Beazley and Maelzer (1998) focus on aspects of their own research activities in order to highlight some of its disabling features. This involved them in a difficult, demanding, critical engagement with their own values, presuppositions and practices. They maintain that from this experience they can now say what good disability research is *not* like.

> For us it should not be embedded in, or regulated by, medical model ideologies; it should not attempt to be neutral or to disregard the impact of oppression on disabled people's lives; it should not reproduce the familiar, and so leave disabling, personal, political or practical barriers unchallenged; it should not exclude disabled people from its process or productions; it should not be controlled entirely by non-disabled people and it should not be reluctant to venture into untapped theoretical and methodological territory. (p. 14)

An important issue that this insightful statement raises, concerns the political commitment on the part of the researcher. This is a research practice that is concerned with the struggle for participation and non-discrimination. Nor does this minimise the demands for 'integrity and a rigorous attitude and approach to one's research' (Blair, 1998, p. 15).

It is important to appreciate that being a researcher is a learning experience involving crucial changes in one's own ideas and intentions. Writing on their experience of a series of seminars held in London in 1991 on the theme of 'Researching Physical Disability' two experienced researchers (Parker and Baldwin, 1992) indicate how their perspectives had been challenged during these meetings and debates:

> there is no doubt in our minds that our research, or rather the way in which we think about our research, has been changed by our participation in these seminars. We started off feeling defensive and resistant to the message we were being asked to heed. . . . This led us to an inevitably painful reappraisal of the work we have done, and are doing, trying to identify the ways in which that might have been, albeit unwittingly, oppressive. (p. 201)

We must not underestimate the contentious nature of these ideas that have been briefly outlined. This can be exemplified by considering the criticism of Hammersley (1998) with regard to what he calls partisan research. He contends that such ideas are based on a 'simplistic sociological theory in which fundamentally there are only two sides – the oppressed and oppressors'

(p. 32). A careful exploration of the writings of disabled people on this question clearly illustrates the complex, multi-faceted and contradictory nature of oppression and in particular, the ways in which class, race, gender and age compound or cushion the impact of such experiences (Begum, 1992; Morris, 1991; Oliver, 1996; and Corker, 1997). It is far from a simplistic perspective that is being advocated by these disabled scholars.

Nor in encouraging the importance of voice are we denying the heterogeneous nature of disability and the ways in which some voices have more prominence than others. One of the issues facing the disability movement concerns the relationship between the individual and the collective including the transformation of the personal into political consciousness. An emphasis on difference with dignity must not lessen the importance of collective solidarity and community. One of the tasks of research is to 'recognise both commonalty and difference in the experience of disablement' (Stone and Priestley 1996, p. 705).

Over the years a series of questions have become perennial concerns in my work in relation to disability research. They include:

• Who is this work for?

• What right have I to undertake this work?

• What responsibilities arise from the privileges I have as a result of my social position?

• How can I use my knowledge and skills to challenge the forms of oppression disabled people experience?

• Does my writing and speaking reproduce a system of domination or challenge that system?

• Have I shown respect to the disabled people I have worked with? (Barton, 1994, p.10)

This list of questions is not meant to be exhaustive, nor am I suggesting that I am beyond criticism in relation to these concerns in my own practice. They do illustrate the sorts of priorities and intentions that I am struggling to implement in my own practice.

## EXTERNAL CONSTRAINTS

However, the question of changing the social relations of research production is much more than an individual issue or even about the context in which the research takes place. One of the crucial factors supporting the existing processes of production are the research funding bodies. They are gatekeepers to the resources which are necessary for research to be undertaken. As such, they exercise an important influence on priorities, possibilities and outcomes of projects. In the seminar which we have previously referred to in London in 1991, one of the outcomes of these sessions was the production of proposed guidelines for supporting disability research. It was agreed that the following statement be sent to all funding bodies with the hope of stimulating some debate:

### Guidelines for Funding Applications to Undertake Disability Research

1. *Defining Disability*

In recent years there has been a move away from the understanding of disability as an individual or medical problem and a move towards understanding disability as the social restrictions confronted by disabled people living in a society which is not organised to take account of their needs. This move has been led by disabled people and organisations controlled by them and takes as its focus a definition which sees disability as 'the loss or limitation of opportunities to take part in the life of the community on an equal level with others due to economic, political, social, legal, environmental and interpersonal barriers' (adapted from the Constitution of Disabled People International). Such a definition conceptualises disability as an equal opportunities issue. All organisations involved in disability research should take this conceptualisation as central and formulate both a statement of intent and procedures and practices commensurate with the formulation or an equal opportunities policy in respect of disability.

2. *The Funding Body as an Organisation*

The funding body should be informed about disability issues in all its activities, i.e. in the context of funding decisions in all areas of research and as an employer.

(a) Disability should be treated as an equal opportunities issue.

(b) Disabled people should be represented on all decision-making bodies concerned with disability research.

(c) The organisation should not seek exemption from the Quota.

(d) The organisation should take all action necessary to enable equal access to all of its activities.

3. *The Funding Body as a Provider of Resources for Research and Development*

(e) The funding body should encourage applications from disabled people and organisations controlled by them.

(f) Appropriate support systems should be established to enable disabled people and their organisations to make successful applications. This would include the provision of clear guidelines to applicants and the establishment of feedback mechanisms where applications are not successful.

(g) The organisation should provide ongoing support to projects which are funded.

(h) The refereeing process should seek to fully involve organisations controlled by disabled people in its procedures.

4.  *Criteria to be Applied by Funding Body to Organisations Applying for Resources*

The applicant organisation should be informed about disability issues in all its activities.

(i) Disability should be treated as an equal opportunities issue.

(j) The organisation should not seek exemption from the Quota.

(k) The organisation should take all action necessary to enable equal access to all its activities.

(l) Procedures for involving disabled people and organisations controlled by them should be integrated into all research proposals from the outset and costings should reflect this.

(m) The funding body will consider whether the dimensions of gender, race, class and other issues of oppression have been incorporated appropriately into the proposal.

5.  *Criteria to be Applied to Individuals Applying for Resources from the Funding Body*

(n) Preference will be given to disabled people.

(o) Where appropriate, individuals will be encouraged to work in partnership with organisations controlled by disabled people.

(p) Criteria (i) and (m) above will apply. (*Disability and Society*, 1992)

We did not receive a single response. Thus, there is still clearly a great deal of hard work to be undertaken and no room for complacency. One of the issues we face when attempting to contribute to changing the nature of research cultures, is that in our enthusiasm we can both understate the problematic nature of some aspects of the new ideas and also become doctrinaire and oppressive. A fundamental feature of the emancipatory approach which needs to be a central factor of consideration is that of self-criticism. This is not to imply that there cannot be deeply felt convictions but they are subject to challenge and change. Thus, the position of the researcher as learner is a fundamentally important one.

The argument provided in this paper must not be taken to imply that disabled people's ideas must be accepted unreservedly or uncritically. Nor as far as I am aware are disabled scholars advocating such a position. Debate and dialogue are essential features of an anti-oppressive approach to social relations including those of research. This is a reciprocal learning experience.

However, we need to consider the cautionary words of Gitlin *et al.* (1992) who maintain that:

> It is not enough to say that research is educative simply because something has been learned, for this ignores who determines what is studied. (p. 7)

This draws our attention to the centrality of the power to define what is significant in the research act and whose interests these definitions serve. If research is to become more enabling in the lives of disabled people then this issue will need to be critically engaged with.

Creating the conditions in which emancipatory research will be able to develop is going to be a difficult and long-term task. Thus, researchers like Zarb (1992; 1997) argue for the importance of a transition process in which participatory research will lead to emancipatory practices. According to Zarb (1997), the former involves disabled people in varying degrees, 'while the latter means that the research is actually controlled by them as part of a broader process of empowerment' (p. 51). The nature of oppression is complex and contradictory and the process of empowerment in the wider struggles of disabled people is reflected in particular ways in the research context.

## CONCLUSION

In this brief paper we have attempted to identify some of the key factors involved in both the prevailing social conditions and relations of research production and that which has become known as emancipatory research. The degree and stubbornness of the difficulties, or more appropriately disabling barriers, that need to be changed in order for this alternative, enabling approach to be realised, must not be underestimated. Part of the task will necessitate engaging with the following sorts of fundamental questions: What does it mean for researchers to give up control? What will academic integrity mean in this context? What is the role of the non-disabled researcher? How do we relate to disabled participants who do not subscribe to a social model of disability? How are disagreements over significant features of the research task to be resolved? How far is there a hierarchy of voices emanating from the disability community? What is involved in listening to such voices? Are particular research methods more appropriate than others in this change process?

As a non-disabled researcher seeking to grapple with these difficult questions, the experience has been disturbing, frustrating, disappointing and an exciting steep learning-curve. Demystifying the research act is crucial, unsettling and liberating.

One of the fundamental tasks in the struggle for empowerment is that of making *connections* between a range of significant factors. It is the sociological imagination that C. W. Mills (1970) identifies as being able to link biographical, situational and wider structural, economic conditions and relations. The particular is important but it must be linked to wider concerns. Thus, in relation to the issue of voice we need to recognise as Giroux (1991) maintains that:

> a politics of voice must offer pedagogical and political strategies that affirm the primacy of the social, intersubjective, and collective. To focus on voice is not meant to simply affirm the stories that students tell, it is not meant to simply glorify the possibility for narration. Such a position often degenerates into a form of narcissism, a cathartic experience that is reduced to naming anger without the benefits of theorising in order to both understand its underlying causes and what it means to work collectively to transform the structures of domination responsible for oppressive social relations. (pp. 54–5)

The task of changing the social relations and conditions of research production is to be viewed as part of the wider struggle to remove all forms of oppression and discrimination in the pursuit of an inclusive society.

## REFERENCES

Abberley, P. (1992) Counting us out: a discussion of the OPCS disability surveys. *Disability, Handicap and Society*, Vol. 7, no. 2, pp. 139–56.

Barnes, C. (1991) *Disabled People in Britain and Discrimination: a Case for Anti-Discrimination Legislations*. London: Hurst and Company.

Barnes, C. (1996) Disability and the myth of the independent researcher. *Disability and Society*, Vol. 11, no. 1, pp. 107–10.

Barnes, C. and Mercer, G. (eds.) (1997) *Doing Disability Research*. Leeds: Disability Press.

Barton, L. (1994) Disability, difference and the politics of definition. *Australian Disability Review*, no. 3, pp. 8–22.

Begum, N. (1992) Disabled women and the feminist agenda. *Feminist Review*, no. 40, pp. 70–84.

Blair, M. (1998) The myth of neutrality in educational research, in P. Connolly, and B. Troyna (eds.) *Researching Racism in Education: Politics, Theory and Practice*. Buckingham: Open University Press.

Clough, P. and Barton, L. (eds.) (1995) *Making Difficulties: Research and the Construction of Special Educational Needs*. London: Paul Chapman.

Connelly, N. (1990) *Raising Voices: Social Services Departments and People with Disabilities*. London: Policy Studies Institute.

Connolly, P. and Troyna, B. (eds.) (1998) *Researching Racism in Education: Politics, Theory and Practice*. Buckingham: Open University Press.

Corker, M. (1997) *Deaf and Disabled or Deafness Disabled*. Buckingham: Open University Press.

Giroux, H. (ed.) (1991) *Postmodernism, Feminism and Cultural Politics: Redrawing Educational Boundaries*. New York: State University of N.Y. Press.

Gitlin, A., Bringhurst, K., Burns, M., Cooley, V., Myers, B., Price, K., Russell, R. and Tiess, P. (1992) *Teachers' Voices for School Change: an Introduction to Education Research*. London: Routledge.

Guidelines for funding applications to undertake disability research (1992) *Disability and Society*, Vol. 7, no. 3, pp. 279–80.

Hammersley, M. (1998) Partisanship and credibility: The case of anti-racist educational research, in P. Connolly and B. Troyna (eds.) *Researching Racism in Education: Politics, Theory and Practice*. Buckingham: Open University Press.

Hargreaves, D. (1996a) Teaching as a research-based profession: possibilities and prospects. London: Teacher Training Agency Annual Lecture.

Hargreaves, D. (1996b) Educational research and evidenced-based educational practice – a response to critics. *Research Intelligence*, no. 58, pp. 12–16.

Mills, C. W. (1970) *The Sociological Imagination*. Harmondsworth: Penguin.

Moore, M., Beazley, S. and Maelzer, J. (1998) *Researching Disability Issues*. Buckingham: Open University Press.

Morris, J. (1991) *Pride Against Prejudice*. London: Women's Press.

Morris, J. (1992) Personal and political: a feminist perspective on researching physical disability. *Disability, Handicap and Society*, Vol. 7, no. 2, pp. 157–67 (special issue).

Oliver, M. (1992) Changing the social relations of research production. *Disability, Handicap and Society*, Vol. 7, no. 2, pp. 101–14 (special issue).

Oliver, M. (1996) A sociology of disability or a disabilist sociology, in L. Barton (ed.) *Disability and Society: Emerging Issues and Insights*. London: Longman.

Oliver, M. (1997) Emancipatory research: realistic goal or impossible dream? in C. Barnes and G. Mercer (eds.) *Doing Disability Research*. Leeds: Disability Press.

O'Reilly, J. and Barot, T. (1997) Woodhead in purge against 'PC' research. *Sunday Times*, 31 August.

Parker, G. and Baldwin, S. (1992) Confessions of a jobbing researcher. *Disability, Handicap and Society*, Vol. 7, no. 2, pp. 197–203 (special issue).

Shakespeare, T. and Watson, N. (1997) Defending the social model. *Disability and Society*, Vol. 12, no. 2, pp. 293–300.

Smithers, A. (1995) *Times Educational Supplement*, 8 September.

Stone, E. and Priestley, M. (1996) Parasites, pawns and partners: disability research and the role of the new disabled researchers. *British Journal of Sociology,* Vol. 47, no. 4, pp. 699–716.

Zarb, G. (1992) On the road to Damascus: first steps towards changing the relations of disability research production. *Disability, Handicap and Society*, Vol. 7, no. 2, pp. 125–38 (special issue).

Zarb, G. (1997) Researching disabling barriers, in C. Barnes and G. Mercer (eds.) *Doing Disability Research*. Leeds: Disability Press.

**4**

# A VOICE IN WHAT? RESEARCHING THE LIVES AND EXPERIENCES OF VISUALLY DISABLED PEOPLE

## *John Swain and Sally French*

### INTRODUCTION

The question in the title, 'a voice in what?', begs a precursor: what is 'voice'? A major theme within *Making Difficulties* (Clough and Barton, 1995) was the notion of the researcher as change agent, and as Barton and Clough (1995, p. 142) state in their concluding chapter:

> This involves the researcher taking the voice of disabled people seriously, listening to them, exploring their lived experience in particular contexts.

The term has various meanings, as reflected in such phrases as 'authentic voice' and 'representative voice', yet it is often not defined in the research literature. There are complex issues in defining the term, not least being whether it refers to an individual or group. The concept of voice is often used to denote collective expression, as in the above quotation which could be taken to suggest that disabled people speak with one voice. For the purposes of this paper, we would use the term in two ways, both of which bridge the individual and the collective. The first is voice as a say in any form of decision-making, planning or evaluation. This can refer both to the power of an individual in relation to others, and also to voice in a collective sense, that is 'democratic voice' through mechanisms such as majority vote, with connotations of the will of the people. The second concept of voice refers to people telling their own stories of themselves and their experiences. Voice in this sense bridges the individual and the collective as it speaks both to the common threads in the lives of, for example, people with visual impairments living in a disabling and disablist society and to differences and diversity in lived experience.

A central question for researchers who invoke the concept of voice, and our particular focus in this paper, is 'a voice in what?' The question is crucial given the criticisms of research by disabled people as being useless in their struggle for full participative citizenship and even, in itself, oppressive both in processes and products (Oliver, 1996). We shall address the question through a retrospective critical analysis of a small-scale project researching the lives and experiences of visually disabled people. In the following section we outline the context by: first describing the project, what we were doing, how and why; and second summarising the current debates in disability research to which we hope an analysis of the project will contribute.


## IN CONTEXT

We were commissioned by a publisher to write a book for 11–14-year-olds about people with visual impairment. The book was to be one of a new series entitled *Understanding Differences*, which was to include texts on racism, gender and disability. This project did not come to fruition. However, four years later (July 1997) the final product, entitled *From a Different Viewpoint: the Lives and Experiences of Visually Impaired People* was published by a different publisher, the Royal National Institute for the Blind (RNIB).

From the outset we were positive about the project and, it has to be said, despite our reservations that we explore here, we retain our original enthusiasm. We had two related starting-points:

1. The book would be written from a social model perspective. We conducted a brief review of texts for adolescents and found, as we suspected, that they espoused a medical, or more general, individual model of disability. A major part of this project for us both personally was the challenge of explaining the social model in a way that was accessible to young people.

2. The book would reflect the views of visually disabled people and, given the social model approach, the views of the Disabled People's Movement.

We undertook this project in the context of far-reaching and complex debates about the nature of disability research in relation to voices of disabled people (in both senses outlined above). These debates have largely focused around the terms 'participatory' and 'emancipatory'. In a previous paper (French and Swain, 1997a), we argued that these two methodological bases can be traced to distinct historical roots. Participatory methodologies have arisen from qualitative research approaches which aim to reflect, explore and disseminate the views, concerns, feelings and experiences of research participants from their own perspective. The realisation of participatory research goes beyond this, however, to engage participants in the design, conduct and evaluation of research, with the construction of non-hierarchical research relations (Zarb,

1992). Participatory research, then, attempts to change the social relations of research processes. Emancipatory research, on the other hand, has its roots in the growth of the Disabled People's Movement and the development of the social model of disability. It is essentially controlled by disabled people from the formulation of research questions to the dissemination of findings, and is realised through changing the social relation of research production (Oliver, 1992). In emancipatory research the social relations of production are conceived as part of the processes of changing society to ensure the full participation of disabled people.

The current debates in disability research need to be understood in the context of broader political debates about the nature of disability and social change. Essentially, to engage in the debates is to recognise that research is not apolitical or disinterested. All disability research is political and interested, and contributes to the construction of 'disability' within society. Claims to participatory and emancipatory research, by researchers, are stances within the politics of disability. The simplest and most challenging question posed for researchers is: whose side are you on?

As Oliver (1997) has shown, researchers have adopted a variety of methodological stances in addressing this ostensibly simple (perhaps simplistic) question. Within his analysis there are four stances: conservative, individualist, situationalist and materialist. However, whilst we accept the direction of Oliver's analysis, that is reflection on the political stance of research, our involvement in this project has led us to question classification systems of research. We should add that we would equally question our own previous analysis of disability research as being participatory or emancipatory. Without denying the contribution of such analyses to understanding the nature of disability research, they divert debate towards research methodology rather than the politics of disability. As Barnes and Mercer point out in relation to emancipatory research, 'It must be "reflexive" and self-critical lest a new orthodoxy is established which turns "doing disability research" into a technical routine' (1997, p. 7). The game becomes one of categorising approaches or research projects, as in our previous analysis, as 'emancipatory' or 'participatory'. To characterise the discourse, it becomes: is this an example of emancipatory research and by what criteria can it be so judged?

From our research experiences, we would endorse Barton's statement: 'intent is no guarantee of outcome' (1996, p. 6). In this light an analysis of research has two related foci: the methodological basis in terms of principles and strategies; and the actual processes engaged in and barriers to realising principles. We shall discuss these first in relation to participatory and then emancipatory intentions.

A third, and we would argue, crucial basis for analysis from current disability research debates, is in evaluation. The realisation of emancipatory and participatory research is through critical reflection on principles and practices. At this level of analysis, categorisation of research as emancipatory or participatory becomes meaningless. Researchers, we, need to confront the contribution of research to social change towards, in general terms, civil rights for all and, more specifically, full participative citizenship for disabled people. We shall conclude this chapter by evaluating this project in these terms.

## NEGOTIATING PARTICIPATORY PROCESSES
### Participatory principles and strategies

At this point we are outlining what we saw as an ostensibly clear basis for realising participatory principles as the foundation before pursuing a more critical analysis.

1. This was an open project with clear aims and an end product. There were, as we saw it, no hidden agendas. The foundations of participatory research must lie within the participants' understanding of the aims, processes and products of the research, both in relation to the project as a whole and their own personal involvement. A seemingly clear basis for explanations was offered as the production of a book with explicit purposes.

2. The book, the product of the research, would reflect the views, concerns, feelings and experiences of visually disabled people. In practice this was achieved through open-ended interviews conducted with individuals and groups. Two groups of young visually disabled people were interviewed, one within a special school and the other within a unit in a mainstream school. Individual interviews were conducted in participants' homes: four young visually disabled people and eight visually disabled adults. Each interview began with an explanation of the project, its aims and processes. This provided the starting-point for participants to explore their experiences and views to be conveyed in a book about visual disability for 11–14-year-olds. All interviews were recorded and transcribed. Using this data, a number of case studies were included and the interviews were used to underpin the whole book.

3. The research participants had some control over the processes and products of the research. Open-ended interviews allowed participants to direct the agenda of their inputs. Furthermore, the main participants received taped drafts not only of their own contributions but of the whole book in draft form, with an opportunity to make suggestions, comments and amendments.

4. The project offered ownership of the product of research. For instance, all the main participants are identified in the book and each of the case studies included a photograph of the participant, chosen and supplied by the participant.

5. The project offered a basis for equity in the relationships between the researchers and the 'researched'. Indeed it could be argued that, in some respects, a role of co-author was constructed for participants through

strategies outlined above. It could be claimed that the 'researchers' and 'researched' had a shared interest in their involvement in this project, providing foundations for a democratic research process.

## Reflecting on participation

We tried to ensure that the young visually disabled people we interviewed for our book were volunteers and that they would not be supervised by their teachers while being interviewed by us. This is an ethical issue as children, like adults, should not be forced to take part in research against their wishes (Ward, 1997a). This did not, however, occur. During both of the group interviews a member of teaching staff was present. One of the group interviews replaced a lesson and the teacher constantly 'chipped in' to ensure that the young people spoke at length – she behaved in her role as a teacher, encouraging people to talk and even commenting on some of the issues they raised. An example occurred when hobbies were being discussed:

| | |
|---|---|
| *Teacher* | Can you tell Sally about your hobby Paul because it is quite an interesting one? |
| *Paul* | I used to be in a motor bike team. I live on a farm, my Dad's a farmer, so I drive tractors and stuff. It's easy. |
| *Interviewer* | Do you think you could manage on the road? |
| *Paul* | Yeah, I'm going to get a motor bike when I'm sixteen. |
| *Teacher* | But you might not be allowed to. |
| *Paul* | I think I will . . . well I don't know. |
| *Teacher* | Nobody's mentioned another hobby that I know a lot of you have . . . computing. |

Another example of the teacher's intervention occurred when discussing what sighted young people should know about visual disability:

| | |
|---|---|
| *Interviewer* | What other things do you think should go in this book for people of your own age who are trying to understand what partial sight is like? |
| *(Silence)* | |
| *Teacher* | If each of you had one sentence to say. Let's go round and you can give one sentence each about what fully sighted children should know. Go on James, you start. |
| *James* | I don't know. |
| *Teacher* | Come on, you can do it. |

We had little control over this situation as we negotiated the interviews without meeting the teachers concerned and were entirely dependent upon their goodwill. The interviews occurred on their territory and in their time. We did not feel we could be demanding as the only reward we offered for their trouble was a copy of the book on publication.

Some of the young people we interviewed did show signs of discomfort. One of us asked a young man whether he felt awkward talking about visual disability and he agreed that he did. Another interview, with Ellen, a young visually disabled woman and her sighted parents, caused embarrassment when the parents went into detail about their daughter's impairment:

| | |
|---|---|
| *Mother* | It's rare isn't it Ellen? |
| *Ellen* | Yes, very rare. |
| *Father* | It's so rare that they haven't got statistics to be able to go by anything. Do you know all the parts of it, can you remember it all? |
| *(Interviewer* | I'm picking up at this point that Ellen is uncomfortable.) |
| *Ellen* | No. |
| *Father* | No, well one was a little extra toe, you were born with an extra toe, weren't you? |
| Ellen | Yeah. |
| *(Interviewer* | I'm feeling terribly uncomfortable at this point. Feeling we're stuck in something I can't control and, more importantly, Ellen can't control.) |

In the school which had a unit for visually disabled pupils, we were told that it would not be possible to undertake a group interview as neither the visually disabled pupils themselves nor the staff identified them as a group. The concept of a group appeared to go against the philosophy of inclusion, at least by the staff, even though the school had a 'special' unit. A group interview did, however, take place without difficulty and, although a teacher sat at the back of the room, he did not join in the discussion. In the school which was specifically for visually disabled pupils, the headmaster, himself visually disabled, wanted to be interviewed too and seemed generally suspicious of our intentions. He was not, however, insistent and did not obstruct the research in any way.

We might have avoided these problems by taking more time and care over organising the interviews. We were, however, working under strict time constraints imposed by the publisher and were entirely unfunded. The publisher did not see the necessity for any interviewing and was satisfied that, as one of us is visually disabled, the book would provide an authentic account of visual disability on that basis alone. The experiences and voices of disabled children have, however, been silenced and ignored and, as Ward points out, 'Disabled children and young people are likely to have different perspectives than those of disabled adults' (1997b, p. 44). The visually disabled adults we interviewed, which including three married couples, were all known to us personally and were not, therefore, representative of visually disabled people generally. They did, however, have varied life experiences.

The interviews were open-ended which allowed the voice of the research participants to be heard. As mentioned above, early and late drafts were sent to many of the participants, in an accessible format, and they were invited to send comments in print, braille, on audiotape or by telephone. Their comments, mostly minor, were taken seriously and the drafts were amended accordingly. One comment, that the international elements within the book were tokenistic, was more difficult to respond to. However, only a few participants responded, and they were all adults. The task we set the participants was quite demanding. In taped form, for instance, simply listening to the book took about three hours. It may be that we could have provided more support during this stage of the project or, as recommended by Ward (1997a), offered payment in the form of a gift voucher. However, in a participatory approach, research participants must always have the option of discontinuing their involvement whenever they wish.

The participants were not, however, involved in the overall planning of the book, the research methodology or the choice of topics presented. The interview material did, however, underpin much of the content of the book and was also used to write six short case studies to illustrate the varied lives and experiences of visually disabled people.

## NEGOTIATING EMANCIPATORY PROCESSES

### Emancipatory principles and strategies

In general terms, while the project at least aspired to a participatory approach, any foundations, in principle and practice, for emancipatory research are more debatable. Certainly the research was not controlled by the democratic voice of disabled people. Nevertheless, our critical analysis of this project has implications for researchers who aspire to emancipatory intentions. Again we identify first emancipatory principles and strategies.

1. The research was controlled by disabled people, in the sense that both authors are disabled. One of the authors is herself visually disabled and has written and spoken on the issues of visual disability, and disability generally, over a number of years. The other author has insulin dependent diabetes, is active in the Disability Arts Movement, and has written about and researched disability issues since the late 1970s.

2. The book espouses a social model of disability. It contains specific chapters explaining the social model, the Disabled People's Movement and Disability Arts, and the whole book is orientated towards presenting the social model in a form which is accessible to the specific audience. As far as we know, it is the only book written for this audience from this viewpoint. A major assumption here is, of course, that a social model of disability can be made accessible to young people, particularly given the dominant disablist ideologies and images. We gave an early draft to two non-disabled young people for their comments and responses.

3. The book disseminates the views of disabled people, through both the interviews and literature by disabled people. The book and the project as a whole was written to promote and further an understanding of disability espoused by the Disabled People's Movement.

4. It could be argued that the emancipatory work of disabled people in providing Disability Equality Training was being developed in a different way

through this book. The book, and the research on which it is based, is expressly politically interested. The orientation towards change is similar to that taken in Disability Equality Training by disabled people in that it attempts to change understanding about the nature of disability, or more particularly to explain the disabling nature of society. The aims of Disability Equality Training can be stated as follows:

(a) to reach a social as opposed to an individual (or medical) model of disability throughout the teaching and learning process

(b) to challenge some of the common misconceptions and false distinctions which relegate disabled people to the status of a discriminated-against minority

(c) to equip participants with a working knowledge of disability which will enable them to recognise the discriminatory language and the visual images that help perpetuate the inequality of disabled people. (Gillespie-Sells and Campbell, 1991)

Though our specific focus was visual disability and the material was directed to an audience not usually addressed by Disability Equality Training, the aims of the book were very much along the same lines.

Our main strategy in realising these aims was through the use of activities in an attempt to engage young people in relating to the issues through their own lives. These activities covered such topics as *Words and Pictures*, *Questions of Charity*, *At Your Leisure*, and *Getting Around*. In developing the activities we drew on the materials and processes of Disability Equality Training. For instance, no use was made of simulation exercises (French, 1996).

5. And, finally, there was the possibility that the project was emancipatory for the participants (including the researchers) by giving voice to their views and concerns and, significantly, disseminating their voice through publication.

## Reflecting on emancipation

Our reflections come from two directions. The first addresses the related issues of who controls and who benefits from the research, focusing on the publishers and then on ourselves as researchers. The second turns to the possible emancipatory nature of the book.

There was considerable shaping of the knowledge by the two publishers whom we dealt with during the production of this book. This included the length, size and style of the book, and the insistence by the first publisher that we include an 'international perspective' for marketing purposes. We did not feel qualified to do this and were initially resistant. Although we did find it interesting, our attempts were somewhat tokenistic; the book is essentially about the lives and experiences of visually disabled people in Britain. We did, however, contact over sixty organisations of and for visually disabled people throughout the world, some of whom sent useful material which we used in the book. We also included case studies of two visually disabled people from India and Malaysia.

The first publisher would not allow us to include activities for the young people to work through although we believed that this would greatly enhance their understanding of the content. The book, being one of a series, had to conform to a predetermined format. The book was eventually 'dumped' by the first publisher (when it was almost complete) for marketing reasons when it appeared that other books in the series would not materialise. There may, however, have been more serious problems as the publisher no longer produces educational books for schools.

We searched for a new publisher for over six months without success. Their comments were always the same; they liked the book but did not think it would sell in sufficient numbers as the National Curriculum is crowded. As Kerton reminds us:

> No-one will publish your book because they like you, because they see it as an act of charity or because they think your words are so meaningful that it's only right and proper for the whole world to hear them. They will publish your book only if they feel sure enough people will buy it to make them a profit. (1986, p. 93)

The publishers suggested that, had the book been about disability in general, rather than visual disability alone, it might have had more scope.

The book was eventually taken on by the Education Services of the Royal National Institute for the Blind (RNIB). Although we were grateful, we did not consider this ideal for a book based upon the social model of disability as the RNIB is an old traditional charity much criticised by some of the people who took part in the research. There was no choice of publisher, however, which led to feelings of vulnerability and some degree of conflict over, on the one hand, satisfying the RNIB, and on the other hand giving a 'true' account (as told by the research participants) and not compromising our own values and beliefs. We were forced to 'tone down' the section on charities though it remains quite critical. The oppressive nature of charity advertising, for example, is discussed as well as the reasons why some disabled people dislike charities. The toning down was basically handled by also providing a more positive view of charities, summarising the range of services they provide and activities they engage in (from information provided to us by the RNIB).

The RNIB also thought some of the material, based on what the interview participants said about their experiences, was too negative. We made no modifications, however, and the point was not pursued. The RNIB allowed the inclusion of activities and considerable lengthening of the book. An optimistic print run of 2,000 copies was made but whether the book will sell in large enough numbers to be profitable remains to be seen.

We entered into considerable negotiation with the RNIB over the photographs in the book, particularly the photograph on the front cover. They wanted us to use the picture 'The Blind Girl' by Millais which we used within the book to illustrate a negative image of blindness. This picture shows a beautiful, sad looking, young woman, in a situation of isolation, with a label reading 'Pity the Blind' hung around her neck (the wording on this label cannot, admittedly, be fully seen in the picture.) Eventually the RNIB followed our idea of using a picture to illustrate the inclusion of visually disabled people in mainstream school.

The book does contain a few photographs that we would not have chosen ourselves, including one which purports to illustrate peripheral vision (one of us has this condition and knows it does not). Negotiations were never closed, but after more than four years we wanted the book to be published without further delay. We felt vulnerable as the person we were working with was leaving the organisation and a recent shortfall in budget had held up production by several months. Most of the pictures in the book do, however, reflect the social model of disability showing, for instance, cluttered pavements, enabling technology and visually disabled people pursuing a variety of occupations and leisure activities.

Negotiation also took place over the title of the book. The RNIB were keen that it should contain the word 'attitudes' whereas we, in line with the social model of disability, wanted a title which reflected far wider concerns. Our title was, however, accepted without great difficulty. The first publisher also made the initial assumption that the book would revolve around attitudes and much discussion was had about the social model of disability in the early stages of production. Despite these problems, our negotiations were not, overall, any more difficult than those we have had with other publishers and in some areas, for example illustrations, we had rather more control than, in our experience, is usual.

We turn next to our own involvement as researchers. Both of us are university lecturers who are expected to write and undertake research. A book for secondary school pupils is not, however, regarded as the best use of our time as it tends to be viewed as insufficiently scholarly, intellectual or academic. In view of this no funding was sought for this project. Such attitudes are another factor which shape the research undertaken and the production of knowledge by academics (French, 1993). This is not to imply, however, that we did not gain personally from writing the book far more than any of the participants are likely to have done. We have another publication to our names (albeit of the 'wrong' type), we have learned a great deal, we have written the chapter in this book, we have spoken at an international conference, and will, if the book sells more than 1,000 copies, receive royalties. As Oliver (1997) has pointed out, researchers and the researched are rarely equal partners and participatory research does little to remedy this situation.

An advantage of having no funding or allocated time from employers, was that we were not beholden to anyone and were relatively free to pursue our own ideas. The lack of time and funding did mean, however, that the ideals of participatory and emancipatory research, which tend to be time-consuming, were only followed through at certain points in the research and writing process. The production of this book has been driven almost entirely by our own motivation and the encouragement of all who took part.

Finally, in relation to possible emancipatory processes in this project, questions can be raised about the effectiveness of this book as a disability equality learning tool. It is debatable, for example, whether such material will be of any use to young people when their visually disabled peers are segregated within special schools or special units within mainstream schools. There are also questions concerning the appropriate use of the book as a means of changing attitudes and behaviour towards visually disabled people. It is unclear, for example, whether the teachers who use the book will be in sympathy with the social model of disability. However, Spender (1981) points out that, in a fundamental way, ideas and research findings which are not in print do not exist and that if we have some interesting ideas and experiences, which may help or be of interest to others, we should try to publish them.

Questions can also be raised about whether non-disabled teachers should be teaching disability equality material at all, or whether this should be left to disabled people themselves. It is possible that the activities in the book may be used together with material which follows an individualistic model of disability; for example, simulation of visual disability as advocated by the RNIB (1991). The RNIB did, in fact, include a list of their own publications under the 'Further reading' section at the back of the book. One is entitled *What You See and What You Do Not See* and another *Eye to Eye: Understanding Visual Impairment*. It is likely that these will take an individualistic approach to visual disability. When ideas and research findings are disseminated researchers and writers lose control of them, the ideas may be taken out of context or applied in ways and to areas not envisaged by the researcher.

Similar arguments surround all disability equality literature and courses (Swain and Lawrence, 1994; French, 1996). Thus despite our efforts at including visually disabled people in this project, it is uncertain whether this will have any real influence on the attitudes and actions of their sighted peers.

## CONCLUSION: AN EVALUATION

We concluded our previous paper (French and Swain, 1997a) by suggesting three questions that need to be addressed by any research in this growing field. We posed them in the belief that all research with people is political, both socially and personally. Whether research is undertaken by non-disabled or disabled people, whether it espouses a social or a medical model of research, it is a personal experience for all the participants (including the researchers). Researchers enter into the lives of others, even if they consider themselves to be 'non-participants' or actually never meet the research participants; for example, when using postal questionnaires. The three questions attempt to address the significance and usefulness of the research from the viewpoint of participants. We conclude this chapter by evaluating our own research in terms of these three questions.

- *Does the research promote disabled people's control over the decision-making processes which shape their lives?*

There are positive answers to this in so far as the project offered visually disabled people control over the literature and images of visual disability. We believe that this should not be underestimated. Given the oppressive nature of dominant images and discourses of disability produced largely by non-disabled people, liberation or emancipation must include a change in the control of production of images and literature (Pointon with Davies, 1997). Our doubts about the effectiveness of this research in relation to this question hinge crucially on the constraints over control. It was a process of negotiation in which interests were played out between ourselves, the participants and other interested parties (most notably the publishers). Ultimately the question can only be answered by disabled people themselves and we have not explored this.

- *Does the research address the concerns of disabled people themselves?*

We would answer, in large part, positively to this question, for reasons outlined above. Though none of the participants spoke explicitly about the social model of disability and none were active members of the Disabled People's Movement, we found that the interviews provided a rich source of examples of barriers faced by visually disabled people. Few of the participants spoke about medical conditions. Again, however, this question can only be answered by our own judgements. Some participants did respond to the draft we sent them of the book, but some did not. Lack of response cannot be taken as agreement. Furthermore, even if the book reflected the concerns of the participants, the sample was entirely opportunistic.

- *Does the research support disabled people in their struggle against oppression and the removal of barriers to equal opportunities and a full participatory democracy for all?*

This, of course, is the most difficult question to answer. That we intended to support disabled people is all we can say. Indeed, as with the above questions, the real answers can come only from disabled people themselves. Reflecting on these questions we conclude that the basic answer to each is 'in intent', and we all know where the path of good intentions can lead.

Basically, it is our experience that the power-relations in the production of research go well beyond the actual participants, including researchers. Research is produced within the social and historical context of the participants' intentions and endeavours. The terms 'participatory' and 'emancipatory' cannot be defined solely by power-relations internal to the research. Research production is a process of negotiation in which interests are played out both between participants and between participants and other interested parties. Participation and emancipation are not categories of research, but processes constructed within negotiated constraints.

## REFERENCES

Barnes, C. and Mercer, G. (eds.) *Doing Disability Research*. Leeds: The Disability Press.

Barton, L. (ed.) (1996) *Disability and Society: Emerging Issues and Insights*. London: Longman.

Barton, L. and Clough, P. (1995) Conclusion: many urgent voices, in P. Clough and L. Barton (eds.) *Making Difficulties: Research and the Construction of Special Educational Needs*. London: Paul Chapman.

Clough, P. and Barton, L. (eds.) (1995) *Making Difficulties: Research and the Construction of Special Educational Needs*. London: Paul Chapman.

French, S. (1993) Telling, in P. Shakespeare, D. Atkinson and S. French (eds.) *Reflecting on Research Practice: Issues in Health and Social Welfare*. Buckingham: Open University Press.

French, S. (1996) Simulation exercises in disability awareness training: a critique, in G. Hales (ed.) *Beyond Disability: Towards an Enabling Society*. London: Sage.

French, S. and Swain, J. (1997a) Changing disability research: participatory and emancipatory research with disabled people. *Physiotherapy*, Vol. 83, no. 1, pp. 26–32.

French, S. and Swain, J. (1997b) *From a Different Viewpoint: the Lives and Experiences of Visually Impaired People*. London: Royal National Institute for the Blind.

Gillespie-Sells, K. and Campbell, J. (1991) *Disability Equality Training: Trainers' Guide*. London: Central Council for Education and Training in Social Work.

Kerton, P. (1986) *The Freelance Writer's Handbook*. London: Ebury Press.

Oliver, M. (1992) Changing the social relations of research production, *Disability, Handicap and Society*, Vol. 7, no. 2, pp. 101–15.

Oliver, M. (1996) *Understanding Disability: From Theory to Practice*. London: Macmillan.

Oliver, M. (1997) Emancipatory research: realistic goal or impossible dream? in C. Barnes and G. Mercer (eds.) *Doing Disability Research*. Leeds: The Disability Press.

Pointon, A. with Davies, C. (eds.) (1997) *Framed: Interrogating Disability in the Media*. London: British Film Institute.

Royal National Institute for the Blind (1991) *Finding Out About Blindness* (Training Pack). London: RNIB.

Spender, D. (1981) The gatekeepers: a feminist critique of academic publishing, in H. Roberts (ed.) *Doing Feminist Research*. London: Routledge and Kegan Paul.

Swain, J. and Lawrence, P. (1994) Learning about disability: changing attitudes or challenging understanding, in S. French (ed.) *On Equal Terms: Working with Disabled People*. Oxford: Butterworth-Heinemann.

Ward, L. (1997a) *Seen and Heard: Involving Disabled Children and Young People in Research and Development Projects*. York: Joseph Rowntree Foundation.

Ward, L. (1997b) Funding for change: translating emancipatory disability research from theory to practice, in C. Barnes and G. Mercer (eds.) *Doing Disability Research*. Leeds: The Disability Press.

Zarb, G. (1992) On the road to Damascus: first steps towards changing the relations of research production. *Disability, Handicap and Society*, Vol. 7, no. 2, pp. 125–38.

# 5

# 'VOICE' IN EMANCIPATORY RESEARCH: IMAGINATIVE LISTENING

## *Jenny Corbett*

### INTRODUCTION

In *Making Difficulties*, Clough and Barton (1995) ask 'What assumptions about SEN/disability do I have which are inevitably present in the way I conceive of the study?' (p. 3). I shall begin by responding to that question and addressing this issue will inform my analysis. From my research in the area of discourse theory and the hierarchies within special education and disability services, I assume that some voices are difficult to hear because of a lack of conventional communication resources, a hesitant or inarticulate delivery and a marginalised social status (Corbett, 1996). My three key assumptions are that:

- the expressions and opinions of powerful professionals talking about disability are listened to with more serious attention than those of disabled people themselves;

- disabled individuals tend to be dislocated from their social context and viewed as inadequate because of personal deficits;

- when professionals speak of 'empowerment' they mean on their terms and using their own perceptions of what is appropriate.

Recognising the obstacles that discourse hierarchies create, I have been looking at the practice of certain professionals who work to help disabled people find 'voice' through their own process of imaginative listening (Corbett, 1998). They were working variously in the areas of special schooling, higher education and disability arts, linked to social service development. For me, their work has provided examples of real empowerment which offers opportunity for autonomy, growth and confidence. It has made me reflect on the capacity for collaboration between empathetic and sensitive professionals working alongside disabled people to develop creative discourses which can be truly enabling. In these instances, imaginative listening led to: children from many special schools being included in art gallery and museum activities; students with learning disabilities being included in a university course; the construction of multi-media profiles in an arts project providing the means to support useful dialogue between service-users and providers.

My focus in this chapter is on two aspects of this development. Firstly, I shall explore how much imaginative listening is being extended to those children and young people who are seen as having moderate learning difficulties and/or challenging behaviours. I see these children as being part of the most numerous and most complex of the special needs groups and those least often listened to with care and respect, perhaps because their behaviour is often provocative and hostile. The second aspect is to consider the social and cultural context in which this imaginative listening is taking place. Without this, I suggest the research remains at a shallow level of analysis, for those labels 'moderate learning difficulty' and 'emotional and behavioural difficulty' have always involved social and cultural dimensions.

I shall begin, therefore, by exploring the concept of 'voice' as it refers to these groups in particular. I shall then ask what it is that makes some forms of research 'emancipatory' in nature. The next section will address individuals in their social context, as an essential element of any approach which involves imaginative listening. Building upon dimensions of research methodology, the use of the video as a potentially emancipatory research tool will be evaluated before I reflect upon possible ways forward.

Whilst the social model of disability has extensively been applied to issues relating to physical and sensory disability and, to a lesser extent, to people with learning disabilities, there has to date been less attention paid to its application to the large group whose behaviour is seen as 'challenging'. I feel that the questions which arise from this inclusion are of considerable interest in exploring our research priorities in the twenty-first century.

## THOSE AWKWARD VOICES

The issue of *voice* in emancipatory research is complex and multi-layered. Firstly, there is a struggle over which discipline (e.g. psychology or sociology) or specific model (e.g. social model of disability) gains prominence in setting the tenor of the research framework and key issues. Secondly, there is a dilemma over selecting a sample and deciding how to listen and what to hear. Finally, and most challenging, there is the need to provide a means of expression beyond the conventional which most accurately conveys the perceptions and experiences of vulnerable people whose apparent ideas are open to interpretive distortion and abuse.

The first element of *voice* is that of academic discipline: where the voice is coming from tends to define the vocabulary to be employed, the theoretical models adopted and the methodological processes to be favoured. In our recent discussion over the key theoretical models which have developed over the last fifteen years in the broad academic field of special education, Brahm Norwich and I reflected that the common assumption among sociologists and psychologists that they were working in very different paradigms and, therefore, were unlikely to find much common ground for research methodology has been challenged in recent examples (Corbett and Norwich, 1997). In their focus upon the child's perspective in assessments by educational psychologists on diagnosis of behavioural difficulties, Galloway, Armstrong and Tomlinson (1994) were using empathetic methods and models familiar to the most sensitised sociologists. Research by Vincent *et al.* (1995), which explored the effects of Local Management of Schools (LMS) on the funding and organisation of special education services and resources, brought together case study and sociological methodology with the perspectives of educational psychologists. Our reflections were that

> it is precisely because the area of education has become so complex and interrelated with political, economic and social issues that connections between the most apposite elements of sociological and psychological perspectives provide the richness of analysis which a separation of the two would lack. (Corbett and Norwich, 1997, p. 384)

One of the key assumptions with which I prefaced this chapter was that the expressions and opinions of powerful professionals talking about disability/ special needs are listened to with more serious attention than those of disabled people themselves. For this very reason, it is vital that those working in applied disciplines like educational psychology become increasingly aware of the differential status and power boundaries within educational discourses and how this impacts upon their vulnerable clients. An excellent example of the way in which professional psychologists are learning how to listen is offered in the recent research by Figg *et al.* (1996). They are a team of educational psychologists working in a socially deprived London borough. Using techniques from discourse analysis, they try to evaluate where they are coming from in terms of their own ways of seeing the world and how this might differ from the views and experiences of the children they work with. They challenge the dominance of a eurocentric psychology, recognising the multi-cultural community whose needs they serve. Their concluding reflections are particularly interesting:

> the Children Act (1989) and the Education Act (1993) with its associated Code of Practice highlight the inclusion of the child's view. Our work suggests that this presents a complex challenge to the educational psychologist. It brings to the fore the issue of the eurocentric bias in many of our psychological theories and the real dilemma for psychologists who need to function effectively and fairly within our developing multilingual and multicultural environment.

There is a need for the profession to continue the debate and our experience would highlight the following areas:

- assessment in context, but whose context?

- competencies, skills and the maintenance of professional standards;

- psychological research and its integration into applied practice;

- representation of minority groups within our profession;

- statutory psychological advice, just who is the client?

- raising the profile of assessment continued professional development as of right – not for self-development but as a process for improving competent practice;

- self knowledge of the EP's own context – both psychological and cultural.
  (Figg et al., 1996, p. 12)

I find this reflective approach to research from educational psychologists to be most encouraging and to challenge all three of my initial assumptions about the nature of research into aspects of special education policy and practice. This is a group of powerful professionals acknowledging their power and recognising their responsibility to listen with more imagination. They know that their professional practice directs them to work extensively from a deficit model of the child as an individual case detached from any social context. By using discourse analysis, they are critical of their own habitual practices and determined to place social context as a high priority within any assessment process. One of my assumptions was that the term 'empowerment' is often used by professionals to impose their views of what is appropriate upon others who may share neither their values nor their experience. This research confronted that reality and presented a real struggle among a team of reflective practitioners to try to see the situation from the child's perspective. It indicated to me that there is an effort to engage in imaginative listening which provides a positive model of really 'emancipatory' research, as I conceive of it within the parameters of how professional practice can continue to learn and improve the quality of its responsiveness.

Goodley (1998), in his research into the role of support staff in day centres in helping to develop self-advocacy skills in people with learning disabilities, is also concerned to ask, 'Are professionals all bad?' He decided that interventions, whilst socially constrained, could also be creative. Where the professional supporting advocacy uses a social model rather than an individual model, they focus upon *capacity (assuming competence)* rather than *deficit (assuming incompetence)*. Gustavsonn (1998) found that in his research of community living among Swedish people with learning disabilities, they recognised professional support as their *right* rather than their *need*. These members of what he termed the 'integration generation' in Sweden were used to receiving support which then helped them to feel they had the ability to cope. What he described as their 'I can' attitude was predicated upon the assumption that the demands of the task in hand and the disposition of the person were balanced by the support and adjustment of professional services. Part of their ability to manage their own lives was their understanding that they could only do this effectively by calling upon the services of others and expecting that certain understandings and allowances would be made to accommodate their learning disabilities. They were very open about their own experience of difference but a *right to services* rather than a *need to services* approach was a powerful tool in their positive self-images. The imaginative use of special support can effectively bridge the barrier between inclusive ideologies and practical daily decision-making.

## WHAT IS EMANCIPATORY RESEARCH?

The term 'emancipatory' research was developed out of extensive debates within the academic area of Disability Studies and involves 'the facilitating of a politics of the possible by confronting social oppression at whatever level it occurs' (Oliver, 1992). Starting from Oliver's definition, I shall explore how I perceive 'the politics of the possible' within the broad assumptions I am using as a frame of reference. My specific focus is upon imaginative listening to young people whose disabilities relate to learning and behavioural problems. This form of listening includes a sensitivity to their social and cultural context. Within the area of emancipatory research there have been many different debates which have included aspects of the following: using the views and opinions of disabled people to design and conduct research projects on disability issues; using disabled researchers; recognising that disabled people have their own prejudices against other oppressed groups and that many experience multiple oppressions relating to gender, sexuality, ethnicity and disability; assessing the validity of disability research which does not improve the quality of life of disabled people; challenging medical models of researching disability issues.

I shall focus on something which is of particular interest to me and which relates to my recent research on the work of professionals with vision (Corbett, 1998). I begin from the premise that powerful professionals have a level of engagement in their own discourse arena which advantages them over the views of those disabled people whose needs they serve. To me, that is a given which is unlikely to change in the immediate future. However, where I feel that social oppression can be confronted by a 'politics of the possible' is in the professionals themselves learning the art of imaginative listening. This process involves the performance of their role, their perceptions and experiences and their capacity to move away from a reliance upon traditional methods. It also involves those who research this process being receptive to the fact that people who may have been oppressive in their practices have the will and the skills to change and adapt. In this sense, I feel that *imagination* is the key to a more emancipatory approach both in the practice and in the research methodology. If I, as a researcher, am ready to put my stereotype of the powerful professional on one side and to become receptive to that person's capacity to really empower and encourage *voice*, then I can record and analyse how they do this and the effect it can have on the child or young person concerned. It requires imagination from the researcher to find examples of imaginative practice among potentially empowering or disempowering professionals.

## UNDERSTANDING INDIVIDUALS IN A SOCIAL CONTEXT

The two specific examples of examining 'voice' which are the focus of this analysis concern expressions from that most vulnerable and often feared group who are variously labelled as having 'moderate learning difficulties', 'emotional and behavioural difficulties' and 'challenging behaviours'. Such young people are not always listened to with respect or trust as their opinions and stories are frequently rejected as lies, confusion, fantasy and inconsequential ramblings. In their recent research into the dilemmas of interviewing children, Moore, Beazley and Maelzer (1998) recognise that the rights of children must come first in deciding how to interview them, what to provide as support structures, the ethics of confidentiality and the specific issues relating to children with various physical or learning disabilities. The interviewer acts as a tool through which 'voice' can variously be released, distorted or inhibited. The professional researcher or support professional may be used as an *active accommodator* to link the person they are concerned to listen to into a dominant discourse which they can then make *actively receptive* to what they have to say. This role as language intermediary is one which requires imagination and skill; without it the gulf of increased inequity gapes.

Both examples which are examined here highlight the negative and dominant image of 'failure' in educational experience and the impact of this upon individual expressions of capability. The notion of *social context* will be explored in two dimensions: the internal concept which individuals have of their own capacities and their own impression of how they fit into the social world built upon their past experiences; the social context in which they are acting out their capabilities in relation to others not labelled as *other*.

The first example is the innovative work of the multi-media project run by Stuart Olesker in the Learning Support Unit which is part of the Centre for Continuing and Community Education in the Faculty of Humanities at the University of Portsmouth. This was selected as an example of imaginative inclusion within the new higher education initiatives (Olesker, Corbett and Ralph, 1997). In presenting the findings of our research, we examined how students with a previous history of being labelled as educational failures, unemployable and incompetent could work sensitively with others to produce high quality drama, film, photography and art. This was a project which had grown over fifteen years from its inception as part of the work of an art college attached to further education provision into an element of higher education provision when the new University of Portsmouth absorbed further education in the last few years. We reflected that:

> This last development has been particularly significant. Suddenly university re-
> sources such as the television centre or a drama studio were available to students
> who for much of their academic and non-academic life had resigned themselves to
> accepting improvised, barely adequate accommodation as apt reflections of their
> marginal status in educational institutions or society. The students on the pro-
> gramme now began to see themselves as others were beginning to see and value
> them: as students in a university. (Olesker, Corbett and Ralph, 1997, p. 27)

In our research focus, we were concerned to look at both what these students were feeling about their abilities in this context and at how Stuart Olesker, their tutor in the project, acted as an *active accommodator* in supporting their self-expression. Thus, we felt that it was important to collect interview data from the students and, to complement this material, to include examples of their completed multi-media creations. We recognised that Stuart Olesker had guided their work by directing from the sidelines, helping the editing process and developing improvised scripts through interactive listening. It was his work as an empowering professional which we were concerned to evaluate alongside the achievements of the students. His 'can do' philosophy inspired the students to overcome their internal labels of incompetence and to flourish in a supportive and creative environment. Although only some of them would continue into degree programmes whilst others would move on to other forms of provision, they had been enriched by the higher education experience for

> the environment of an institution of higher education, offering open lectures to the
> widest range of students, can be of enormous advantage to students discovering
> the delights of exploring new subjects, themes and ideas beyond the realms of
> 'training' or NVQs. The Portsmouth experience suggests that the presence of
> students with a wide range of learning styles and needs in an institution of higher
> education can enrich both students and institution alike. (Olesker, Corbett and
> Ralph, 1997, p. 28)

Had we used interview data alone, many of the students would have emerged as nervous and hesitant. They were in the process of re-evaluating their nega-tive self-image and the one-to-one focus of an interview could serve to rein-force an individual deficit model by highlighting anxiety, incoherence and confusion. By including the edited video material in our data analysis we were able to show what these students were capable of producing in collaboration with their ally and supporter, in the form of Stuart. His great skill was to demonstrate to the students what they were really capable of creating, when they let go of their self-images of failed identities. This approach moves right away from the prevailing emphasis in schooling upon academic achievement as a competitive race between unequal individuals. Rather, it encapsulates inclusivity in bringing together a wide range of students from the learning support unit and from various humanities courses to work within collaborative, co-operative and community values to produce a group presentation. It is about moving away from individual failure towards community achievement: valuing learning as more than just competencies.

## THE VIDEO AS AN EMANCIPATORY RESEARCH TOOL

Reflecting on the methodology for this research project, the use of video as a means of data collection was emancipatory in that it demonstrated the 'can do' capability whilst also confronting the diverse nature of this student sample, whose only shared past experience had been one of lack of confidence. By collecting filmed interviews of the very same students who were then seen performing in video dramas or creating animated films, we could observe how effectively they had used video resources to present powerful and positive images of themselves. In so doing, they were able to challenge their failed identities. We used video data as researchers but we also were involved in evaluating how Stuart was using video editing to help the group gain the satisfaction of producing high quality results.

The second example of observing individuals in a social context focuses more specifically upon children whose behaviours are seen as extremely challenging. In January 1998 four ten-year-old primary-school boys were brought into the crown court of the Old Bailey and charged with the sexual assault of a ten-year-old girl classmate during the lunch-hour in the school toilets. They were acquited after a three-week trial. As I observed the proceedings from the public gallery, it emerged that the broad social context was that their difficult class in a troubled school was located on a council estate which had experienced many problems. The girl who was the alleged victim was on the special educational needs register, had been excluded several times for fighting with children and teachers and was seen as 'at risk' generally. It is beyond the scope of this chapter to examine the wider issues in this example, other than to look at how the video was used as an emancipatory tool.

In this case, as in other court cases where young children are involved, a video screen was used to connect the alleged victim, who was sitting in another room, to the barristers, jury and judge in the courtroom. The woman judge used the video to control the process by which this vulnerable individual presented her argument. This was a child who was used to having her story challenged as a lie or a fantasy. In her discourse encounters with powerful professionals like teachers, she was accustomed to being in trouble. Her views and opinions were not usually treated seriously in the social context of her daily life. As was pointed out to her by the barristers in court, when the police and social workers were 'nice' to her she enjoyed the unfamiliar encouragement. In using the video as a tool for cross-examination, the very sensitive woman judge ensured that this girl was protected from the degrading experience of being exposed to public gaze when she regularly broke down in tears. As soon as this started, the judge switched off the video, blanking out the screen. She then gently suggested to the girl that she could have a little rest. Even when one of the defence barristers asked the judge to leave the video on long enough for the jury to see the girl's 'demeanour', the judge would not comply with this request. The rights of this child to appropriate respect were paramount. Through this empathetic approach this judge made a very stressful experience manageable for this child, who visibly came to trust her and asked her to intervene on her behalf several times when the questions from the barristers became too confusing, difficult or demanding.

I found it interesting, as an educational researcher, to be observing this process in a courtroom rather than the more familiar territory of a school or college classroom setting. It made me reflect that powerful professionals are in a position where they can really make a significant difference to the experiences of the most socially vulnerable individuals when they are entering frightening new discourse arenas. The gap between this child's experience of the world and the complex courtroom debates was a chasm of different languages, meanings, nuances and codes. This woman judge effectively acted as an intermediary: linking this frightened child to the language in which she found herself immersed; translating elaborate sentences for her; asking barristers to simplify their questions and control their body language; and, all the while, calming the child in a gentle tone to reassure her, showing her that she would be treated with care and consideration.

A high court judge is perhaps one of the *most powerful* professional roles. In this example, the power was employed to support rather than to alienate. The child was guided through the minefield of an unfamiliar and potentially dangerous discourse arena and gently shielded from its hazards by an expert protector whose overall control brought this most vulnerable of participants through a fearful ordeal.

## CONCLUDING SUMMARY

To conclude, I need to return to the three key assumptions with which I began: that powerful professionals are listened to more than disabled people; that disabled people are usually dislocated from their social context and seen as failed identities; that when professionals speak of empowering people, it tends to be on their terms and using their own view of the world. I find it difficult to believe that the dominant role of professional discourse is soon going to be substantially challenged by the disability movement. However, I do find that there are examples of effective and imaginative professionals who help those they support to enter the discourse arena with some chance of being listened to with respect.

In my first example, it was Stuart Olesker as a lecturer at a new university who encouraged the students he worked with to see themselves as capable and creative and help them to let go of their negative labels from their experience in compulsory schooling. His emphasis on shared learning experiences and the value of collaborative, co-operative group work was an imaginative way of forging success and promoting confidence. In my second example, it was a woman judge in a court at the Old Bailey who protected and supported a vulnerable girl to tell her own story in her own way.

Both these examples of imaginative professionals concern the issue of 'voice'. They both became discourse conduits through which these uncertain and marginalised 'voices' could speak and be heard in unfamiliar social settings. In researching their professional practice, it required an imaginative use of methodology which was receptive to finding 'voice' in new arenas, not just those of educational institutions. It also included a realisation that 'voice' is about emotional climate, trust, respect and sincerity, without which sounds from the margins can remain unheard or ridiculed as defective.

## REFERENCES

Clough, P. and Barton, L. (eds.) (1995) *Making Difficulties: Research and the Construction of Special Educational Needs*, London: Paul Chapman.

Corbett, J. (1996) *Bad-Mouthing: the Language of Special Needs*. London: Falmer.

Corbett, J. (1998) *Special Educational Needs in the Twentieth Century: a Cultural Analysis*. London: Cassell.

Corbett, J. and Norwich, B. (1997) Special needs and client rights: the changing social and political context of special educational research. *British Educational Research Journal*, Vol. 23, no. 3, pp. 379–89.

Figg, J., Keeton, D., Parkes, J. and Richards, A. (1996) 'Are they talking about us?' (How EPs describe the views of children). *Educational and Child Psychology*, Vol. 13, no. 2, pp. 5–13.

Galloway, D., Armstrong, D. and Tomlinson, S. (1994) *The Assessment of Special Educational Need: Whose Problem?* London: Longman.

Goodley, D. (1998) Staff are bad: the social model of disability and professionals working with people with learning difficulties. Paper presented at 'Policy, Failure and Difference' Seminar, University of Sheffield, 13–15 February.

Gustavsonn, A. (1998) The politics of defining difference – Swedish experiences. Paper presented at 'Policy, Failure and Difference' Seminar, University of Sheffield, 13–15 February.

Moore, M., Beazley, S. and Maelzer, J. (1998) *Disability Research Issues*. Milton Keynes: The Open University Press.

Olesker, S., Corbett, J. and Ralph, S. (1997) Inclusive practices in higher education: an example of imaginative provision. *The Skill Journal*, no. 59, pp. 26–9.

Oliver, M. (1992) Changing the social relations of research production. *Disability, Handicap and Society*, Vol. 7, no. 2, pp. 101–14.

Vincent, C., Evans, J., Lunt, I. and Young, P. (1995) Policy and practice: the changing nature of special educational provision in schools. *British Journal of Special Education*, no. 22, pp. 4–10.

# 6

# 'ONCE UPON A TIME': TEAMWORK FOR COMPLEMENTARY PERSPECTIVES AND CRITIQUE IN RESEARCH ON SPECIAL EDUCATIONAL NEEDS

## Hazel Bines, John Swain and John Kaye

### SITTING COMFORTABLY?

If the terms and justification of research in the study of special educational needs could ever be taken for granted, the grounds for such complacency have been increasingly eroded. The problematising of areas under study was, indeed, the aim of the first volume edited by Clough and Barton (1995). The comfortable rug of neutrality and assumed progress through research are being pulled away, through questions of who benefits and the development of more self-critical approaches to research. Research is not a process which is somehow separate from an existing reality of special educational needs but is in itself a construction of reality.

As Clough and Barton suggest in their concluding chapter, there seems to be a collective voice, a consensus, in *Making Difficulties*. It speaks, perhaps most centrally, to the articulation of many voices, individual and group, to ensure people's views, feelings, perspectives and stories are told, whilst recognising the accounts are constructed in particular social contexts and power hierarchies. It is from this that our present analysis of voice begins, that is as both the articulation of viewpoints through research and a say in the decision-making in research processes.

The purpose of this chapter is to reflect critically on some of these key issues by looking at the stage of planning and access in the early days of a project designed to examine the processes of reorganisation, and the substantial moves towards integrated provision for pupils with special educational needs in one LEA.

## WHOSE STORY?

In a sense, the story of any research starts long before the involvement of the researchers, that is in the social and historic context that gives rise to the research. A story begins with storytellers, however, and as researchers, we began by recognising an opportunity to propose a research project. The immediate context was a proposed reorganisation of special needs provision in one LEA which was intended, as emphasised in public statements and documents disseminated by the LEA, to enable a 'significant reduction in the level of segregation'. In the tables of statistics, this LEA has one of the highest levels of segregation in the country with over 2 per cent of pupils attending special schools.

Our negotiations as researchers began in formulating a proposal with which to approach the LEA. To an extent this was not problematic, as we shared the consensus of *Making Difficulties*. Some basic principles and strategies were relatively easy to formulate.

1. The research would reflect the voices of all participants, including researchers, with particular priority given to disabled pupils as a collective voice.

2. A participative methodology would be pursued and the research would be designed at every stage through consultation with LEA representatives and research participants.

3. The research would engage in processes of change and would focus on the stated principles underlying the reorganisation and their translation into practice.

For us as researchers, then, this was an opportunity to explore the development of provision for young people in mainstream schools who would previously have been educated in special schools, and also to develop a research team committed to 'a sensitive and self-conscious research practice' (Clough and Barton, 1995, p. 143). But the danger is, of course, that this begins to sound like the same old fairy story of research, with a narrative based on the modernist, humanitarian view of research as an unquestionable source of progression. It is the view which is dominant in Higher Education as researchers and would-be researchers seek money, time and other resources to pursue possible openings, opportunities and professional interests.

We begin to construct a different story of research, however, if we begin with the question 'In whose interests is this story being told?' As soon as we stepped into the arena, power-relations and structures in the production of research began to be constructed. The foundations for non-democratic research are beginning to be laid. For example, who sets the process in motion? Three researchers from higher education who need to produce themselves as researchers, and who need to compete for funding. Whom do they approach to initiate negotiations? It was, of course, the policy-makers, that is the people who have most say and power in the process of reorganisation. Rather like the familiar themes of the traditional fairy tale, here are the usual starting-points of a research process that in its funding, conception, conduct and reporting will tend to maintain the status quo and be a mechanism of social control. Even simply to conduct research is, potentially at least, to provide a rationale for this reorganisation, whatever its limitations, and to perpetuate notions of 'special'.

It is in this light that we have conducted our critical reflections in the initial planning and setting up of research processes, looking particularly for a possible basis for open and democratic research in a context which is, initially at least, of necessity non-democratic, and seeking both theoretical stances and methodological approaches which would help us to implement most effectively our aims and ethos.

## FINDING THE SCRIPT

Different views about the nature of social reality underlie the widely differing ways in which social scientists seek to investigate and generate knowledge about the social world. This, however, is not in any way a straightforward relationship and there are no clear strategies for linking the tenets of theory and the methods of empirical research. It is a problematic area for any research in the social sciences, characterised by dilemmas and disagreement rather than certainty. The following analysis of the methodological basis of the present study explores three sets of interrelated issues:

1. investigation of the views of participants and the interpersonal processes through which participants construct meanings and social order

2. the relationships between research design and theory, particularly in terms of the historical, socio-political and ideological context of the research

3. research as a constructive and interactive process and a reciprocal shaping of social theory and action.

As is central to qualitative research generally, this study of participation in decision-making involves an examination of the ways in which people make sense of, create, shape and negotiate the decision-making process. However, the limitations of a thoroughgoing qualitative approach have been the subject of much contention in the literature. In terms of the aims of the present study, the questions concerning the limitations speak primarily to the analysis of the historical and social context of participation in decision-making. As Angus states:

> the view that a satisfactory explanation of social situations may be derived from theories that are 'grounded' in the very situation to be explained obscures the

connections between such situations and wider social structures and power relationships. (1986, p. 72)

Questions of power in relationships are, or course, central here. It can be argued, as by Hargreaves (1986), that a qualitative approach can illuminate the processes of negotiation, showing the construction of power through interpersonal interaction. Yet within such processes of negotiation, participants differ in their power to impose their meanings, their definitions of situations, their 'facts' on others. 'Facts' which are seen as self-evident to participants are in part a reflection of structures and ideologies serving the interests of some people over others, that is the interests of dominant groups. As recognised by Barton (1988), the assumptions and expectations underpinning daily interactions contribute to the creation of special educational needs.

There are two related propositions here. First, processes of negotiation, to use Bernstein's (1976) words, 'presuppose a structure of meanings (and their history) wider than the area of negotiation.' In other words, there is a social reality and there are 'social facts' external to each participant's reality, beliefs and actions. Second, the notion that theory can emerge from and be grounded solely in data, collected in natural settings and unaffected by the values and preconceptions of the researcher, is highly problematic. Qualitative approaches can offer an inadequate basis for addressing the ways in which participation in decision-making is constrained and shaped within wider social structures and power-relations. Furthermore, all knowledge claims are inextricably tied to the satisfaction of human purposes and desires, and an ahistorical, asocial, 'neutral', 'objective' stance on the part of the researcher is illusory.

There are tensions between a commitment to grounded theory and the use of grounding or a priori theory. It is from such tensions that Lather argues for 'dialectical theory-building that aspires to focus on and resonate with lived experiences and, at the same time, is convinced that lived experience in an unequal society too often lacks an awareness of the need to struggle against privilege' (1986, p. 262).

The present study is being conducted on the basis that underlying assumptions are made explicit and clarified at the outset. This question of an a priori theory, which addresses the complex interplay between the personal/interpersonal and the wider structural and ideological power-relations in society, takes us into the realm of critical social science and the emancipatory interest.

The development of the methodological implications of critical social science has taken a number of guises in the literature, including 'research-as-practice' (Lather, 1986) and 'critical ethnography'. The latter is defined by Masemann as follows:

Critical ethnography refers to studies which use a basically anthropological, qualitative, participant-observer methodology but which rely for their theoretical foundation on a body of theory deriving from critical sociology and philosophy. (1982, p. 1)

In the realm of critical social science, this 'body of theory' speaks not only to the relationship between theory and research, but also to the essential nature of theoretical positions. Thus, the notion of 'theory' eschews neutrality and is seen in itself as a political endeavour. To quote one of the early proponents of critical theory:

> the theory never aims simply at an increase of knowledge as such. Its goal is man's (sic) emancipation from slavery. (Horkheimer, 1972, p. 245)

Participants' views and the received 'facts' and definitions of the situation cannot be taken at face value or given equal weight, as in relativist interpretations in which there are as many 'realities' as there are participants. An a priori perspective provides the foundation for illumination and interpretation of data. In an historical overview of the Frankfurt School of Critical Theory, Giroux states:

> One begins not with an observation but with a theoretical framework that situates the observation in rules and conventions that give it meaning while simultaneously acknowledging the limitations of such a perspective or framework. (1983, p. 11)

However, the central danger of a grounding theory is what Lather (1986) calls 'imposition and reification on the part of the researcher'. She calls for meanings to be constructed through negotiation with research participants, for reciprocity between researchers and participants, for research processes that empower participants to understand and change their situation, and for dialectical theory-building rather than theoretical imposition.

In general, such democratisation has been a significant trend in research design (Hall, 1981), yet procedures necessary to attain true reciprocity still remain at a tentative stage of development. Tripp (1983) states that his paper on 'coauthorship and negotiation' in interviews is 'rather a description of a point of departure than of a destination' (p. 44). His search is for 'a research design strategy which recognises and acts upon the power relationship between the researcher and the researched' (ibid., p. 32). We would like to pursue this path in our present project. Our theoretical and methodological concerns therefore focused particularly on how we could involve participants and ensure their voices were heard.

## VOICES OF STORYTELLERS

### Pupils' voices

In what senses is it possible to involve pupils as participants in democratic research? Here, it would seem, are the greatest barriers to participation in the decision-making both within the research process and in the education system. The discrimination against the voices of children is institutionalised and legitimated not only in the role of schools but also by the dominant ideology of 'childhood' in contemporary western society. It therefore comes as little surprise when Armstrong states that

> most previous research into the processes of special education, including that which has sought to investigate how special education serves to reproduce and legitimate aspects of the social structure, has chosen to ignore the child's perspective on these processes. (1995, p. 79)

However, there are possibilities for participatory research. Ward (1997), for instance, has documented processes of participatory research and consultation with young disabled people, particularly following the Children Act 1989. Notwithstanding the effectiveness of the strategies and techniques developed by Ward and others, there are clearly particular barriers to the democratic involvement of young disabled participants at this point within our project. Most obvious is that there is no such group of young people, in the sense that the reorganisation has yet to happen and thus none of the young people to be affected by the reorganisation have been identified. The group is, at present, merely a statistic! Furthermore, many young people involved will perhaps never identify themselves as such, that is young people who, following the reorganisation, remain in mainstream schools rather than being placed in a special school.

Without denying the possibility of participatory research with pupils who participate later in the research, there clearly need to be other mechanisms of involvement if the interests of the client group are to be represented in the research processes at this early stage. We see three possibilities, all of which involve seeing the eventual participants in the research as part of wider spheres of interests.

First, it could be argued that the interests of young people in special education should be represented by disabled people, and in particular by the Disabled People's Movement. This, it could be argued, provides for a democratic voice of people whose lives have been most affected by the provision of segregated education. Special educational provision plays a major role in the segregation and marginalisation of disabled people in this country. We see this as a dilemma. On the one hand is the notion that emancipatory research is controlled by, and for, disabled people (Oliver, 1993). In this light, a voice in the research project could be seen as no more than piecemeal participation in research ultimately controlled by and for the researchers and policy-makers. Yet, on the other hand, a project of this nature which aspires towards a democratic approach cannot deny the democratic voice of disabled people. We are approaching a local organisation of disabled people to discuss these issues.

Second, such interests could be seen to be represented by the pupils in the LEA who are presently attending special schools. It may well be possible to pursue this as many young people in special schools and colleges within the LEA have in recent years been involved in a project organised by a local self-advocacy organisation (French and Swain, 1977). The existing networks could thus be drawn on to identify pupils who could represent the views of those presently in segregated, special education. One argument against this approach would be that the focus of the research is on those receiving education in mainstream schools. The counter-argument is that this is only an administrative division which is further rationalised and strengthened by the reorganisation. Again, we shall approach the self-advocacy organisation to discuss the issues.

The third possibility is the involvement at the planning stage of pupils with special educational needs already in mainstream schools. Our strategy here is the formation of focus or advisory groups. In her review of relevant research, Ward (1997) suggests that it is more appropriate to have a separate consultative group of young disabled people which can focus on the particular aspects of the research which concern and interest them. The group, rather than individual interviews, may provide a better forum in which young people feel freer to participate and comment.

Thus there are at least some possibilities for ensuring a strong democratic voice representing the interests of pupils in the decision-making that shapes the research process.


## Teachers' voices

Handy (1993, p. 292) suggests that change is 'a necessary condition of survival,' and that within organisations there will be useful and natural differences which are necessary for their improvement and survival. The LEA in our project is moving towards a policy to reduce the numbers of children within special schools. This reflects some of the major points in the Green Paper (DfEE, 1997) which aims to increase the level of inclusion. Demands will be made on the teachers and other professionals in both mainstream schools and those transferring from special schools. In looking at how they adapt their practice to accommodate the changes, it will be crucial that teachers' voices are articulated.

Rapid changes in the educational system have created an enormous amount of anxiety for teachers and other professionals. Galloway (1989) was concerned about the adverse effects on teachers of meeting further demands asking, 'Who defines the needs of teachers?' (p. 86). Recent reforms have put increasing pressure on schools and the support services for SEN. The 1993 Education Act introduced the need for schools to have a written policy for children with special educational needs. In their commissioned research on schools' policies for SEN, Tarr and Thomas (1997) indicate that two-thirds of policies examined outlined the school's commitment to integration as an ideal but lacked detail. SEN policies will therefore need to be reviewed. The role of the SENCO in schools will also have to be reviewed within the reorganisation. The Code Of Practice (DFE, 1994) extended the workload of SEN teachers.

Lewis (1997) report that in secondary schools SENCOs are becoming more involved in managerial, non-teaching roles. They report a mixed reaction to this change in direction. They also identify a number of different types of teachers involved in the education of children with special educational need, such as 'core' or full-time SENCOs, part-time teachers, support or 'periphery' workers and peripatetic or 'non-resident' teachers who act as SENCOs in a small number of primary schools.

Class and subject teachers also have a very important part to play in the reorganisation. There may be teachers who are delighted with the new philosophy and changes, whereas others may feel disappointed with advancement, have been demoted, moved sideways and have problems in adapting to the new structures. Teachers with varying degrees of expertise and experience will have different views on integration. Vlachou (1997) reports on the differing perceptions of teachers to integration. Teachers were positive suggesting that integration offered increased socialisation, and broadened the children's experience and their own in attitudinal responses to disabled people in the community. She reports some contradictions and even the same teacher may have different interpretations of integration. Thus the voices of teachers cover a wide range of different viewpoints, depending on their role and understanding in relation to the perceived changes.

## Policy-makers' voices

Research which includes the voices of policy-makers has to consider both the position of such participants and how their roles are conceived. Although, ideally, the views and interests of policy-makers should be congruent with those of the users of services, policy analysis has rightly identified that policy-makers have their own vested interests and values. As a result, it is now common to polarise the interests of policy-makers and clients, with the former being seen as having both the desire and the power to impose their definitions and plans upon the latter. In addition, policy-makers (and often the professionals who implement the policies) have also been regarded as agents of the national or local state, and of society, consciously or unconsciously replicating and exacerbating the oppressions of social inequalities and discrimination in areas like SEN.

Research on SEN which includes an explicit policy dimension, particularly if committed to critical, social perspectives, is therefore likely to be framed by a strongly critical, even hostile, stance towards policy and policy-makers. However, research ought to include some evaluation of the appropriateness of such conceptions. Whilst recognising that much policy is inimical to the interests of those it apparently seeks to support, and that policy-makers and professionals do act in pursuit of their own vested interests, it is important to recognise that recent educational reform has made the policy map much more complex, with many competing and conflicting interests and pressures. In particular, notions of policy-makers may need to be redefined, to include not only politicians and legislators, administrators and practitioners, but also parents, school governors, the media and students/pupils, recognising that there may be pressures on policy-makers themselves from groups who have been either newly empowered by recent reform and its accompanying discourses of consumerism, or who are empowering themselves through social movements which stress the perspectives, and the rights of decision-making, of those for whom policy was traditionally enacted.

This is particularly well illustrated in research which, conducted at local level, and focusing on locally conceived change, is likely to identify LEA personnel as key policy-makers, albeit within a national policy context. Whilst acknowledging the importance of being critical of LEA policy-making, LEAs are a good example of policy-makers subject to a range of pressures, including attacks by central government on their legitimacy, redefinitions of their role by the Audit Commission and schools empowered by LMS, and demands from parental pressure groups. Such pressures are particularly evident in relation to SEN and illustrate some of the contradictions inherent in policy-making and implementation.

It therefore seems important to ensure that whilst retaining a critical stance towards both the generation and implementation of policy at local level, research should be sensitive to such pressures and should explore how these impact. At the same time, we need to recognise that there are structural power-relationships between the different participants in the research. A democratic methodology should both allow the policy-makers to speak for themselves and also enable their views to be interrogated by others, including parents and pupils. We will have to consider ways of doing this.

STORY THEMES

As noted earlier, grounding theory can be problematic in terms of making research truly reflective of different voices. It is therefore crucial to make assumptions explicit and construct a dialectical interplay between the views of participants in the research. This is not simply a methodological issue, though as explored above, methodological design and intentions are crucial in ensuring critical and participatory research. It is equally important to consider those themes which are likely to dominate the story as told in the different voices of participants. This is particularly necessary when conducting research which is concerned with policy implementation, since such change is especially likely to have a range of dominant themes and associated discourses associated with trends in policy at the time of the research. In addition we all bring certain personal theoretical conceptions and assumptions to research, which need to be made explicit.

We have therefore also spent time considering some of the likely policy and theoretical themes in this research. This has included locating the research in some of the explicit and implicit educational and social assumptions about desegregation and inclusion, and considering what critical perspectives we might need to adopt.

The policy objectives of the reorganisation which we are researching have been clearly stated to focus on inclusion. However, definitions of inclusion do vary and involve various moral, political, social and educational aims and assumptions (Clark *et al.*, 1997; Sebba and Ainscow, 1996). In addition, more traditional notions of integration, following from the Warnock definitions of locational, social and functional integration (DES, 1978) continue to inform policy, with few real changes in the level of segregation in the UK (Swann, 1988; CSIE, 1992). Although most countries are concerned to desegregate their provision in some way, such change may be based on a variety of rationales and mechanisms (Pijl, Meijer and Hegarty, 1996; O'Hanlon, 1995; Thomas and Loxley, 1997).

As researchers working in this area, therefore, we need to consider carefully both our own and other research participants' definitions and perspectives. For example, is the focus on integration or inclusion? Does it largely comprise relocation from special to mainstream settings or is it acknowledged and expected that the wider curricular and organisational changes associated with inclusion should occur? And what are the conceptions, and aims, of the pupils, parents and professionals involved? Our research should be concerned to articulate possibly different and even contradictory perspectives. We will also try to avoid taking for granted some of the assumptions in existing analysis of integration and inclusion, in particular that it is dependent on particular factors or indeed that it is generally beneficial to pupils and schools.

We also need to draw on the more challenging critiques of special education that have developed from sociological analyses, and from the social model of disability espoused by the Disabled People's Movement. The former has raised questions about the dominant humanistic and educational justifications of segregated provision:

> In whose interests did special education actually develop – was it more in the interests of the mainstream system which was provided with a 'safety valve'? (Barton and Tomlinson, 1981, p. 19)

The Disabled People's Movement has taken the discourse of integration and inclusion beyond relocations, policies and practices within education into the politics of disability and the fight for Civil Rights:

> In such a struggle, special, segregated education has no role to play. (Oliver, 1996, p. 94)

From this standpoint, the dominant ideologies of integration, in particular, have themselves come under critical analysis, suggesting that the provision of inclusive education for all involves changes that go well beyond the policies and practices usually subsumed under the umbrella of 'integration'. As Vlachou states:

> the philosophy underpinning new policies in regard to the context, form, structure and implementation of the curriculum excludes any serious consideration of inclusive education. (1997, p. 34)

Such viewpoints have, then, laid the foundation for a critical analysis of integration in any research into special needs provision.

There are also some other important themes to consider. Policy and provision for special educational needs is being located increasingly within more general policies for education. Having been incorporated, however marginally at first, into the curricular and governance frameworks established by the 1988 Education Reform Act (Bowe and Ball, 1992), it has also been subject to marketisation and managerialism (Bines, 1995b) and is now being explicitly linked to current government concerns over educational standards (DfEE, 1997).

Policy changes by LEAs will be strongly linked to such themes, particularly since their functions, whilst now recognised again under this government, become increasingly subject to formal evaluation and accountability (Ofsted, 1997). The extent to which concerns such as equity can be pursued within such policy contexts may be problematic (Bines and Thomas, 1994). Our research will need to consider carefully how the broader policy contexts, and specific local policy intentions, interact, as well as critically interrogating policy assumptions on the relationships between educational achievement, school management and resources as they affect special educational needs. In focusing on the perspectives of pupils and professionals, as well as policy-makers, we will also be questioning the processes of policy implementation.


## A TEAM OF STORYTELLERS

Issues related to who makes policy are also relevant to who makes research. There has tended to be a polarity between research conducted about policy, often on behalf of policy-makers, and research which deliberately eschews such perspectives and interests by focusing on giving voice to, and empowering, the 'researched'. Much research, however, also reflects tensions along this continuum, either because of funding and access issues and/or because of theoretical needs. We concur with Riddell, Brown and Duffield (1995) that policy research should not be avoided because of such tensions. Indeed there are strong arguments for engaging with research which focuses on either a particular policy initiative or policy aspects in more general terms.

Nevertheless, there remain some fundamental issues of definition and power. For example, for us, as for many researchers working on policy changes, access negotiation has started with policy-makers such as LEA personnel, as the gatekeepers to topic, settings and participants. This may be the research reality but nevertheless affirms certain systems of power and control. It also suggests that policy-makers are the most significant partners in any attempt to extend the research 'team' beyond those who originally thought of the research. It is crucial therefore in research which is committed to working with the range of participants that other informants and representatives are sought for the 'team', and in particular that such contributors are not exclusively education professionals of one sort or another.

Finally, we have also had to consider the working of the 'core' research team, namely ourselves. One of our strongest methodological reasons for our working as a team is centred on the potential value of bringing researchers with different perspectives and experiences together to both complement and correct the inevitable partialities of perspective and theory characteristic of any researcher. For example, we hope that the strengths of Swain in relation to undertaking participatory research with young people will be balanced by, and correct some of the partiality of, research conducted by Bines which has tended to focus on more general aspects of policy and on the interests of policy-makers and professionals (Bines, 1995a; Swain, 1995) and that Kaye will in turn contribute a particular approach to the perspectives of professionals. The definition of the research has been a critical factor as we each enter the team with our own frames of reference. To date we have been able to synthesise our conceptions of issues and methodology, but cannot assume this will always be the case. There will be ideological and personal interactions to resolve in future. However, at least by working as a team we have attempted to overcome some of the individualised and competitive culture of research in higher education.

At the same time we all have a common interest in 'producing' research as part of our work. As such it will be important to ensure that this does not prevent us making alliances between ourselves and the individuals and groups involved in their research. As research becomes even more of a commodity, particularly in higher education, maintaining a participatory approach increasingly becomes a significant and problematic aspect of the research process. This is highlighted in the production of academic publications, including this chapter, which are controlled by, and for, researchers.


## A HAPPY ENDING?

It seems pertinent to conclude by asking what we anticipate in this research on which we are embarking. It seems to us that there is a central contradiction which will be the dynamic and tension in the construction of the story of this research. On the one hand the research will provide a forum for dialogue and discussion, directed and constructed by both the researchers and participants. This, it seems to us, is central to any research which aspires to be 'democratic' in a participative sense. We see this as a formative process in which people's (researchers' and participants') views are not only expressed and recorded, but are actually formed, clarified, challenged, re-formed and created through discussion. The terms of the research, particularly special educational needs and inclusion, will be particular foci for critical reflection.

On the other hand, the research processes will be defined and constructed within the very power structures and relations they purport to illuminate and critique. Democratic research has to be purposefully constructed in the face of institutionalised discrimination and hierarchical power-relations. It is in this light that priority must be given, as positive discrimination, to the voices of disabled pupils. But at this point we can only ask whether the dominant discourses of integration/inclusion and special educational needs will preclude the telling of new stories, and whether the tale told of the research itself be one of still making difficulties.

## REFERENCES

Angus, L. B. (1986) Research tradition, ideology and critical ethnography. *Discourse*, Vol. 7, no. 1, pp. 61–77.

Armstrong, D. (1995) *Power and Partnership in Education: Parents, Children and Special Educational Needs*, London: Routledge.

Barton, L. (1988) The politics of special educational needs: an introduction, in L. Barton (ed.) *The Politics of Special Educational Needs*. London: Falmer Press.

Barton, L. and Tomlinson, S. (eds.) (1981) *Special Education: Policies, Practices and Social Issues*. London: Harper and Row.

Bernstein, R. L. (1976) *The Restructuring of Social and Political Theory*. Oxford: Basil Blackwell.

Bines, H. (1995a) Risk routine and reward: confronting personal and social constructs in research on special educational needs, in P. Clough and L. Barton (eds.) op. cit.

Bines, H. (1995b) Special educational needs in the market place. *Journal of Education Policy*, Vol. 10, no. 2, pp. 157–71.

Bines, H. and Thomas, G. (1994) From bureaucrats to advocates? The changing role of local education authorities. *Support for Learning*, Vol. 9, no. 2, pp. 61–7.

Bowe, R. and Ball, S. J. with Gold, A. (1992) *Reforming Education and Changing Schools*. London: Routledge.

Clark, C., Dyson, A., Millward, A. J. and Skidmore, D. (1997) *New Directions in Special Needs*. London: Cassell.

Clough, P. and Barton, L. (eds.) (1995) *Making Difficulties: Research and the Construction of SEN*. London: Paul Chapman.

CSIE (1992) *Segregation and Inclusion: English LEA Statistics from 1988 to 1992*, Bristol: CSIE.

DES (1978) *Special Educational Needs (The Warnock Report)*. London: HMSO.

DFE, (1994), *Code Of Practice on the Identification and Assessment of Special Educational Needs*. London: DFE.

DfEE (1997) *Excellence for All Children*. London: HMSO.

French, S. and Swain, J. (1997) Young Disabled People, in J. Roche and S. Tucker (eds.) *Youth in Society*. London: Sage.

Galloway D, (1989), The special educational needs of teachers, in L. Barton (ed.) *Integration: Myth or Reality.* Lewes: Falmer.

Giroux, H. A. (1983) *Critical Theory and Educational Practice.* Victoria: Deakin University Press.

Hall, B. L. (1981) The democratization of research in adult and non-formal education, in P. Reason and J. Rowan (eds.) *Human Inquiry: a Sourcebook of New Paradigm Research.* Chichester: John Wiley.

Handy, C. (1993) *Understanding Organizations,* Harmondsworth: Penguin.

Hargreaves, D. (1986) Whatever happened to symbolic interactionism?, in M. Hammersley (ed.) *Controversies in the Classroom.* Milton Keynes: Open University Press.

Horkheimer, M. (1972) *Critical Theory.* New York: Seabury Press.

Lather, P. (1986) Research as praxis. *Harvard Educational Research,* Vol. 56, no. 3, pp. 257–77.

Lee, R. and Lawrence, P. (1991) *Politics At Work.* Cheltenham: Stanley Thornes Publishers.

Lewis, A., Neill, S. R. St.J. and Campbell, R. J. (1996) *The Implementation of the Code of Practice in Primary and Secondary Schools: A National Survey of the Perceptions of Special Educational Needs Coordinators.* London: National Union of Teachers.

Masemann, V. L. (1982) Critical ethnography in the study of comparative education. *Comparative Education Review,* Vol. 26, no. 1, pp. 1–15.

Ofsted (1997) *LEA Support for School Improvement.* London: Ofsted.

O'Hanlon, C. (ed.) (1995) *Inclusive Education in Europe.* London: Fulton.

Oliver, M. (1993) Re-defining disability: a challenge to research, in J. Swain, V. Finkelstein, S. French and M. Oliver (eds.) *Disabling Barriers – Enabling Environments.* London: Sage.

Oliver, M. (1996) *Understanding Disability: From Theory to Practice.* Houndmills: Macmillan.

Pijl, S. J., Meijer, C. J. W. and Hegarty, S. (1996) *Inclusive Education: a Global Agenda.* London: Routledge.

Riddell, S., Brown, S. and Duffield, J. (1995) The ethics of policy-focused research in special educational needs, in P. Clough and P. Barton (eds.) op. cit.

Sebba, J. and Ainscow, M. (1996) International developments in inclusive schooling; mapping the issues. *Cambridge Journal of Education,* Vol. 26, no. 1, pp. 5–18.

Swain, J. (1995) Constructing participatory research: in principle and in practice, in P. Clough and L. Barton (eds.) op. cit.

Swann, W. (1988) Trends in special school placement to 1986: measuring, assessing and explaining segregation. *Oxford Review of Education,* Vol. 14, no. 2, pp. 139–61.

Tarr, J. and Thomas, G. (1997), The quality of special educational needs policies: time for review? *Support For Learning,* Vol. 12, no. 1, pp. 10–14.

Thomas, G. and Loxley, A. (1997) From inclusive policy to the exclusive real world: an international review. *Disability and Society,* Vol. 12, no. 2 , pp. 273–91.

Tripp, D. H. (1983) Coauthorship and negotiation: the interview as an act of creation, *Interchange,* Vol. 4, no. 3, pp. 32–45.

Vlachou, A. D. (1997) *Struggles for Inclusive Education.* Buckingham: Open University Press.

Ward, L. (1997) *Seen and Heard: Involving Disabled Children and Young People in Research and Development Projects.* York: Joseph Rowntree Foundation.

# 7

# FROM EMANCIPATORY RESEARCH TO FOCUS GROUP: PEOPLE WITH LEARNING DIFFICULTIES AND THE RESEARCH PROCESS

*Sheila Riddell, Heather Wilkinson and Stephen Baron*

## INTRODUCTION

In their introduction to an earlier edited collection, *Making Difficulties: Research and the Construction of Special Educational Needs*, Clough and Barton wrote:

> Critical reflection on the relationship between self and the research process involves exploring and exposing the hidden and taken-for-granted aspects of the social relations of research production. Reflective self-awareness over the methods, commitments, excitements, anger and mistakes of the research act are elements of this task. (Clough and Barton, 1995, p. 4)

In this spirit of critical reflection, this paper offers an account of our attempts to involve people with learning difficulties in a research project undertaken as part of the ESRC's *Learning Society Programme*. As the disability movement has grown in influence, questions have been asked about the nature of disability research and its contribution to the lives of disabled people. Indeed, commentators like Abberley (1987) have maintained that most research on disabled people, rooted within a medical model of disability and focusing on individual deficit rather than social barriers, has contributed to their oppression rather than liberation. As an alternative to these oppressive practices the idea of empancipatory research has been suggested as a way in which the voice of disabled people might be heard and some examples, predominantly with people with a physical impairment, have been offered (Zarb, 1992). Less attention has been paid to the conditions under which emancipatory research is possible and, crucially, whether research in conditions which fall short of this is therefore oppressive. In this paper we want to move beyond such a 'splitting' of the field to offer a more variegated analysis of disability research.

We will review briefly current thinking on what counts as legitimate disability research. We argue that debates on appropriate methods are not merely technical questions, but hinge on disputes regarding the nature of disability, the relationship between activists and the academy and on wider questions of epistemology concerning the basis of social knowledge and theory. In particular, we suggest that the relationship of people with learning difficulties to research shows the relations of emancipatory research to be more complex than often suggested. Parallels are drawn with feminist research where similar debates are waged in relation to how research should be done, who should do it, what counts as evidence and the basis of theory. Having mapped the terrain, we then describe our initial goals in relation to the involvement of people with learning difficulties in our project and discuss how things worked out in practice. Overall, we feel we failed to fulfil our ambitious goals of sharing ownership of the research, but we believe we are now able to comment more critically on the way in which people with learning difficulties are able to be involved in a range of areas of research including theory generation. Above all, we wanted to avoid the sloppy and sentimental view that what is often described as 'giving disabled people a voice', suggesting an act of generosity, automatically improves the quality of their lives.

## RADICAL SOCIAL MOVEMENTS, POWER AND EMPOWERMENT

When radical social movements develop, they are likely to question not only taken-for-granted social arrangements but also the knowledge base which underpins common-sense assumptions about how the world works. In the 1980s, a spate of writing questioned the nature of feminist research and there are perhaps some lessons to be learned about the direction feminist research has taken. A minimum requirement of feminist research is that it should not simply be *on* women but rather *for* women (Duelli Klein, 1983), although what this means in practice, and where research on men fits in, remains a moot point. Qualitative work is not necessarily more feminist than quantitative work (Scott, 1984; Morgan, 1981), since the image of the intrepid male researcher bringing back news from the mean streets may well exclude the experience of women. What matters, the 1980s feminist argument went, is the way in which qualitative work is conducted. Ann Oakley (1981) pointed out that the conventional textbook method of avoiding interaction with the interviewee to prevent data contamination was simply not feasible when discussing highly personal subjects such as the experience of childbirth. Oakley captures very well the absurdity of responding to women's questions in the prescribed textbook manner which advises that:

such questions as: 'Which hole does the baby come out of?' 'Does an epidural ever
paralyse women?' And 'Why is it dangerous to leave a small baby alone in the
house?' should be met with such responses from the interviewer as 'I guess I
haven't thought enough about it to give a good answer right now', or a head-
shaking gesture that suggests 'that's a hard one'. (Goode and Hatt, 1952, cited by
Oakley, 1981, p. 48)

Oakley concluded that feminist social research requires that:

> the mythology of hygienic research with its accompanying mystification of the
> researcher and the researched as objective instruments of data production be
> replaced by the recognition that personal involvement is more than dangerous bias
> – it is the condition under which people come to know each other and to admit
> others into their lives. (1981, p. 58)

Action research, controlled and directed by the research subjects, was regarded
by some as the purest form of feminist research; a frequently cited example of
this was a German study of a women's refuge (Mies, 1983) in which sociologists collaborated with refuge residents in collecting and interpreting life histories. Most feminist research, however, did not conform with this particular
model. Some feminists, notably Stanley and Wise (1983), took an even
stronger line in terms of the generation of theory and control of the research
process. They attacked Marxist feminists for imposing their own interpretations on other women's experience and were particularly critical of the notion
of false consciousness as deeply patronising of other women's experience.
Instead of there being one objective social reality, they claimed, there are
'competing views and realities competently managed and negotiated by members of society', a view which has, of course, been taken up more recently by
those adopting a postmodern perspective (Stronach, 1996). The only way to
do feminist research, Stanley and Wise contend, is:

> to make the researcher and her consciousness the central focus of the research
> experience. (1983, p. 49)

Even though most feminists did not follow this prescription for ethically acceptable research, nonetheless debates about the nature of feminist research
illustrate the dangerous ease of assuming the prescriptive moral high ground, a
tempting position also for those engaged in disability research. As we shall see
from a later discussion, feminists and those working from a social model
perspective agree in their approval of action research as, potentially, the most
democratic, although such research does tend to be rather thin on the ground.
But there are also interesting divergences; many feminists have moved towards
a relativistic position focusing on recognition of difference (Phillips, 1997;
Young, 1990) and this has led to the neglect of the project of economic redistribution and of research which would contribute to this project (Fraser,
1997). Work in the area of disability, by way of contrast, still tends to reflect
the social model with its Marxist underpinning and there are calls for more

research to explore the implications of complex and divergent identities (Shakespeare and Watson, 1997; Crow, 1996).

## DISABLED PEOPLE, IDENTITIES AND THE RESEARCH PROCESS

Research is clearly not a neutral activity, but may be used to support or subvert dominant social discourses. In Oliver's view, research in the area of disability has hitherto been a conservative rather than a radical force. He comments:

> Disabled people have come to see research as a violation of their experience, as irrelevant to their needs and as failing to improve their material circumstances and quality of life. (1992, p. 105)

In developing a more democratic disability research paradigm, two strands have emerged, participatory and emancipatory research. The distinction between these is not altogether clear; sometimes the terms are used interchangeably and at other times participatory research is seen as a stepping stone towards emancipatory research. French and Swain (1997), for example, argue that the key difference lies in their contrasting relationship with the social model of disability:

> Emancipatory research espouses a social model of disability where the foci for research are the physical and social barriers within society which prevent disabled people leading full and active lives. Although participatory research may give support to the social model of disability, it is not inherently associated with it. In emancipatory research the research processes themselves and the outcomes of research are part of the liberation of disabled people – that is, part of the process of changing society to ensure their full participation and citizenship. This is not just a process of empowerment as in participatory research, where research participants may be given opportunities to tell their own stories and analyse their own situation, but in terms of disabled people taking control of the research processes which shape their lives. The processes and products of emancipatory research are used by disabled people as tools towards the achievement of their liberation. Emancipatory research is thus a form of educational and political action. (1997, p. 28)

Stalker (1998) summarises the main beliefs of emancipatory and participatory research thus:

> First, that conventional relationships, whereby the researcher is the 'expert' and the researched merely the object of investigation, are inequitable; secondly, that people have the right to be consulted about and involved in research which is involved in issues affecting their lives and, thirdly, that the quality and relevance of research is improved when disabled people are closely involved in the process. (1998, p. 6)

Fulfilling all three criteria in action research with physically disabled people is imaginable and such research has provided the model for all disability research. Attempting to fulfil these criteria with other groups, in our case, people with learning difficulties, is more complex: the expertise of the researcher (presumably the warrant for any research activity) is not transmissible to some people with cognitive impairments; the involvement of people with learning difficulties in the process of the research may similarly be limited; current models of the consultation and involvement of people with learning difficulties in issues affecting their lives suggest that the pulls either to the trivial or to the professionally stage-managed are hard to resist.

According to Stalker, adopting a more democratic research paradigm with people with learning difficulties is potentially problematic for academics because such research, when done properly, is likely to take longer and lead to different forms of dissemination and publication. These requirements run counter to the current intensification of research production, demanding that work is conducted more rapidly and that publications should be in the most prestigious academic journals rather than those aimed at non-academic audiences. The following questions concerning power differentials, Stalker suggests, should be tackled by all those doing disability research but will be particularly tricky for those working with people with learning difficulties:

> how much does – or can – most research 'empower' people with learning difficulties, and in what ways? How many people want to be empowered by research? Or is it the researcher who is empowered, if the study yields more publications or leads to another grant? (1998, p. 6)

These questions are challenging not only for those who perhaps do not make great claims for their work in terms of its empowering properties, but also for those who might be tempted to make glib assertions that their work is 'giving disabled people a voice', without considering whether this is in their gift, whether disabled people wanted it in the first place and what the nature of the gift relationship is. We explore such issues of involving disabled people in the next section.

## ACTIVISM AND THE ACADEMY: INVOLVING DISABLED PEOPLE IN RESEARCH

If, as French and Swain suggest, the social model of disability is associated with emancipatory research, it is perhaps not surprising that the examples of full participation following the removal of barriers generally relate to those with physical and not intellectual impairment. For instance, Zarb (1992) describes an investigation into a self-operated care scheme in which the Greenwich Association of Disabled People played a central role throughout the research, recommending methods of investigation, commenting on research instruments, contributing to the analysis of the data and finally scrutinising the research report. The involvement of the group, according to Zarb, was both 'daunting and exciting'. They 'challenged almost every aspect of the report –

interpretation and inferences, the language used, and even the ordering of the authors' names on the cover.' (p. 137)

Zarb's comments raise important questions in relation to the involvement of disabled people, including those who are multiply disadvantaged, in research. What happens, for example, when researchers and disabled people disagree about the conduct and meaning of research? Do non-disabled researchers ever have the right to disagree with disabled people over how data should be read?

Unsurprisingly, researchers have come up with different answers to these questions. For Barnes (1996) the independence of the researcher must always take second place to the promotion of arguments in support of the struggle of disabled people against oppression, the nature of which he takes to be unproblematic:

> If disability research is about researching oppression, and I would argue that it is, then researchers should not be professing 'mythical independence' to disabled people, but joining with them in their struggles to confront and overcome this oppression. Researchers should be espousing commitment, not value freedom, engagement, not objectivity, and solidarity, not independence. (1996, p. 110)

Shakespeare (1996), on the other hand, sees a separate role for activists and researchers because of the different nature of political and sociological knowledge:

> Disability Studies is an academic investigation of the social world, and as such is more than simply common sense (Giddens, 1989). Sociological discourse is a critical discourse, but also a reflective discourse, because it is critical upon itself. In this, it differs from political language. (1996, p. 118)

Because of the distinction between academic work and political struggle, Shakespeare maintains that he feels accountable to his research subjects in terms of honesty about research intentions and methods, but not to the British Council of Organisations of Disabled People, to local self-organised groups or to other organisations within the movement.

In relation to people with learning difficulties, a particular form of accountability is advocated by Booth and Booth (1993). Their version of accountability is closer to the position of Barnes than Shakespeare, in that responsibility to research participants as well as the wider disability movement is acknowledged. Nonetheless, the type of research described by Booth and Booth does not involve people with learning difficulties in its conduct or in the development of theory. A biographical profile is presented of Molly Austin, a mother with learning difficulties. Molly lives with her two children and her partner Kevin in a dreary and uncomfortable caravan and is about to sign over responsibility for the children to her husband. The authors present two contrasting accounts of Molly, one based on a deficiency and the other on a capacity perspective. Seen through a deficiency lens, Molly appears 'incapable of living up to her responsibilities as a mother or of putting her children's needs before her own' (p. 388). Adopting a capacity perspective, on the other hand, reveals Molly as lacking motivation rather than skills, an understandable response to 'the daily grind of a life cramped by poverty' (p. 390). Support from health and social services is sparse and crisis-orientated. In sum, it is not so much that Molly has failed as that she has not been given a chance to succeed. Given the growing number of parents with learning difficulties, the authors suggest that health and social services must avoid the presumption of incompetence, the mistake of false attribution and the tendency to blame the victim. By highlighting the differing interpretations arising from a capacity as opposed to a deficiency perspective, the authors alert researchers to the dangers of adopting the latter uncritically and suggest that a capacity perspective is more likely to encourage the growth of services which support rather than punish. The work of Tim and Wendy Booth, highlighting barriers rather than individual deficits, appears to be compatible with the social model of disability, although it does not involve disabled people as researchers. Nonetheless, as we shall see in the following section, some commentators would see such work as falling short of the ideal, in which disabled people control all aspects of the research process.

## PEOPLE WITH LEARNING DIFFICULTIES AND THE RESEARCH PROCESS

Stalker (1998), citing Walmsley (1994), refers to the vision created by the social model of disability in which people with learning difficulties oversee a research project from beginning to end, taking the lead role in design, conduct, analysis and dissemination in the same way as the Greenwich Association of Disabled People, referred to above. According to the social model, this should be possible if certain disabling barriers are overcome. In the literature, however, it is evident that there are still few examples of research which have begun to move in this direction, let alone achieve this goal. Here, we consider some recent accounts of the involvement of people with learning difficulties in research projects and the significance of the nature of their inclusion and exclusion.

Townsley (1995), for example, described the way in which researchers at the Norah Fry Research Centre involved a group at a resource and activity centre in an investigation of issues around gender in service provision. Assisted by a group worker and a researcher from the centre, the group devised questions for a questionnaire survey and were involved in the administration of the questionnaire and the collation of findings, which were subsequently presented at a dissemination conference. Similarly, direct involvement of adults with learning difficulties in service evaluation is reported by Whittaker, Gardner and Kershaw (1990). A researcher from the King's Fund Centre (Andrea Whittaker) worked with two consultants (Simon Gardner and Joyce Kershaw) from People First, an organisation run by and for people with learning difficulties with a strong commitment to self-advocacy. Interviews with service users were conducted by Gardner and Kershaw, assisted by Whittaker, who endeavoured to support the consultants without influencing the substance of their questions or their responses. It is interesting that both these examples focus on concrete issues to do with service delivery, where people with learning difficulties will clearly have an active involvement, rather than more abstract or theoretical ideas which might, for example, form the basis of an ESRC research project. Nonetheless, they have little to say about the process of data analysis, in particular the way in which a narrative emerged from the interview transcripts. Nor are we told of any problems which might have arisen during the course of the work concerning the relationship between the supporter and the consultants. Did everyone involved in these projects share similar views of the project, how much of a steering role did the supporters take and to what extent was the work judged by the academic criteria of 'accuracy, effectiveness and consistency' to ensure 'quality and integrity' (Shakespeare, 1996, p. 117)?

Stalker (1998) points out that when researchers encounter difficulty in involving people with learning difficulties in aspects of academic research, there may be a temptation to 'rubbish' research. For example, Minkes, Townsley and Weston (1995) maintain that it is important to focus on issues from service users' point of view and not 'some hidden agenda of ivory towered scientific rigour'. Stalker comments:

> There are some interesting unspoken assumptions underlying this statement. While few would disagree with the first part of it, there is an anti-intellectualism or anti-academicism within the second part which gives pause for thought. Good research is rigorous. It does not follow that rigour is incompatible with a focus on users' viewpoints. (Nor am *I* implying that research carried out in non-academic settings is less than rigorous.) (1998, p. 16)

Stalker describes in some detail the power-relations inherent in her own research; she highlights the points at which involvement of people with learning difficulties was successful and the reasons why, on occasion, it failed. In a research advisory group on a study of the exercise of choice by service users, for example, she comments on the problems encountered by the people with learning difficulties in contributing to discussions. Academic debate on methodological issues, a perfectly legitimate topic for the advisory committee (of which two of the current authors were members), was impenetrable not only to the two consumer representatives but, it later transpired, to the local authority officer as well. It was also difficult for the disabled people to comment on practical aspects of the research since it was not being conducted in an environment with which they were familiar. The presence of a supporter to intervene on their behalf, with the aim of interpreting and refocusing the discussion, might have proved a significant help in removing barriers. The lessons from this experience, suggests Stalker, illustrate certain steps which researchers could take to involve people with learning difficulties in research, but also indicates that there may be aspects of research in which not everybody has the necessary knowledge and skill to play a role. If people with learning difficulties are to be involved in the research, then it should be in ways which draw on their expertise and specialist knowledge, with accountability remaining a guiding principle. Certain types of theorising may be difficult to engage with, but this is an argument not for ditching the theory (she makes the telling point that both the social model and normalisation have made a significant contribution to the improvement of disabled people's lives), but for thinking through where involvement is possible and fruitful and in addition, what is the likely impact of the development of certain theories on people's lives.

To summarise thus far, it is evident that there is currently much debate in the area of disability over power-relations in research. Parallels with the development of feminist research have been drawn, with the suggestion that the loss of confidence in meta-narrative and the identity politics and research accompanying this may have limited the power of the women's movement as a political force. Within discussions of disability research, it is often suggested that disabled people should ideally control all aspects of the research process, with researchers putting their knowledge and skills at the disposal of disabled people rather than acting independently. The possible implications of this for people with learning difficulties have been flagged up: if people's intellectual impairment means that their involvement in research, in particular abstract theorising, is limited, does this mean that the activity should be abandoned and would this contribute to the social marginalisation of this group? It was with the commitment to involve people with learning difficulties in research, but with reservations about the simple empowerment model, that we formed a research group as part of an ESRC-funded project. Let us now look at what happened in practice.

## THE RESEARCH PROJECT AND THE RESEARCH GROUP

The project, entitled *The Meaning of the Learning Society for Adults with Learning Difficulties,* part of the ESRC *Learning Society Programme,* aims to map the education, training and employment opportunities for people with learning difficulties in Scotland, to explore the professional discourses of a range of providers and to understand the perspective of service users of different ages and in urban and rural settings. In order to pursue the latter aim, thirty case studies of people with learning difficulties in two local authorities, involving ten visits to each person, were planned. Central theoretical concerns were the operation of markets and choice, the nature of adult status and the barriers to full social participation. In our proposal we recognised the importance of the involvement of adults with learning difficulties in the research process and undertook to explore 'creative and multiple ways in which this can happen' (Riddell, Baron and Stalker, 1995). Because of the difficulties discussed above in attempting to include people with learning difficulties in a project advisory group (Stalker, 1998), we decided that we would involve a small number of case study participants in the conduct of the research.

There were a number of different ways in which we could have involved adults with learning difficulties and we spent a considerable amount of time thinking through the various possibilities. One possibility was to train people with learning difficulties to act as interviewers but there were a number of problems with this. Our methodology did not involve the use of a one-off structured interview, but rather a series of ethnographic interviews entailing progressive focusing. In the tight timetable to which we were committed, we did not have enough time to train people with learning difficulties to act as interviewers and also were uncertain about the implications of using people with learning difficulties in this way. Certainly we did not wish to assume that there was some essential quality in having an intellectual impairment which specifically enabled people with learning difficulties to empathise with each other in a way which others could not. The work involved an ongoing process of theorisation which any inexperienced interviewer would have found difficult to undertake. Within the context of this project, then, we could see few benefits and a number of significant disadvantages in involving people with learning difficulties in the wider fieldwork.

Another possibility, the one we finally pursued, was to bring together a group of people with learning difficulties who had already participated in the case studies and involve them in discussion of the initial research findings and of key themes within the research. Rather than considering the abstract concepts referred to above, we decided to focus on lower order constructs arising from our initial inductive analysis of the qualitative data. These were broadly connected with various life experiences including childhood and going to school, leaving school and moving on, work, money, homes and housing and relationships. Although much less ambitious than some of our earlier plans, this nonetheless proved both difficult to implement and rewarding. The achievements and difficulties of the research group are discussed below.

The group consisted of six people, two women and four men aged between 19 and 59, who had participated in the case studies and were subsequently invited to participate in the research group. They all lived in a large Scottish city and meetings of the group were held in an adult resource centre on a two-weekly basis. At the time of writing, seven meetings of the group had taken place and more were planned. Getting all six people together proved to be difficult. Each was travelling to the centre from a different location using public transport and so times of arrival were unpredictable. The people who attended the research group were involved in a range of other activities which sometimes took priority. The effect of this was that most meetings lacked one or two participants. Most people in the group knew each other either from school or from attending events for people with learning difficulties; this familiarity produced a relaxed atmosphere, but also led to the surfacing of some long-established tensions. The group was convened and supported by Heather Wilkinson with Sheila Riddell acting as observer.

There was some uncertainty, reflected in frequent discussion at team meetings, of the priority which should be accorded to the work of the research group and how it should relate to the main body of the research. In the event, we invested a considerable amount of the project's resources in the research group, spending one day a week of the research fellow's time in co-ordinating and convening the group over a twelve-month period. Most of the case study individuals in the first stage of the ethnographic work participated in the research group and in this sense there was a sense of continuity between its activities and the main research project. At the same time, however, we were conscious of a permanent state of tension between the amount of time we were able to dedicate to the group and the rest of the study. Group members made it clear that they would have welcomed the opportunity to meet up with the researcher on an ongoing and regular basis, and again there were tensions between individuals' need for friendship and the nature of the research relationship. Some of the less secure group members asked Heather Wilkinson frequently if it would be possible to get together outside the planned research meetings and it was difficult for Heather to explain that this was not possible.

The ideal referred to earlier, where people with learning difficulties decide on an issue which needs to be researched and convene a group of researchers to help them in this task, was far from the reality of this research group. In formulating our proposal to the ESRC to undertake research as part of the *Learning Society Programme*, we had drawn on ongoing work with people with learning difficulties (Baron, Gilloran and Schad, 1995a, 1995b; Stalker, 1997). However, as it did not then exist, the research group had not been involved in the formulation of the project and the research questions, and so it was not surprising that they regarded the research as our project in which they were temporarily involved. They were happy to come along to the meetings because they enjoyed the interaction with the researchers and each other, but they expected the researchers to structure what happened when they arrived. They also made it clear that they expected the sessions to be reasonably entertaining and not too much like hard work. They were not keen on interviewing each other because they preferred the discussion to be co-ordinated by the researchers, whom they regarded as new and interesting people in their social world. This was not to imply that they accepted passively the direction suggested by the researchers; if they felt the topic was boring or irrelevant they would steer the conversation back to an area of greater interest. They also reminded the researchers of their relatively privileged position. For instance, it was suggested to Heather Wilkinson that she was very lucky having her job because it appeared to be well paid and spending time talking to them was scarcely difficult.

## LEARNING DIFFICULTIES AND THEORY

As indicated earlier, we wished to explore the extent to which people with learning difficulties were able, within the context and limitations of our project, to participate in theory generation. Based on our knowledge of the people who attended the research group and our reading of others' experiences, we did not seek directly their views on the nature of choice, the meaning of adult status or their views of themselves as users and consumers of services. Rather, we engaged in a discussion of their common-sense theories and the implications of these for the provision of education, training and employment services. As well as listening to their views, we told them about some of the ideas emerging from the data and they in turn commented on these. In the following sections, we discuss two major areas where the research group contributed to the generation of theory.

### The identity of people with learning difficulties

The focus of our research is the experience of people with learning difficulties as members of what is optimistically termed a learning society. Our definition of people with learning difficulties is deliberately fuzzy, based on operational definitions employed by service providers including government agencies, voluntary organisations and user groups. One of the aims of the research group was to encourage those within it to reflect on their collective experience as people with learning difficulties. However, it became apparent that the subjectivity of group members was not based on the idea of being a person with learning difficulties and indeed this was not an identity they welcomed.

This rejection of the term was first apparent in early discussions as to who should be invited to the group. Fiona, one of the participants, expressed opposition to including two of the men because they could not read and write and therefore would not be able to make a valid contribution. Rejection of the identity of a person with learning difficulties was evident throughout Fiona's discussion of her educational experiences. She described how she had enjoyed her first primary school where she had learnt to write, won prizes for Bible work and joined in playground games. Then she had moved to a special school which she described as

> the type of school where you didn't have a lot of friends.
> I felt they were all special needs, I didn't have any friends as such. . . . I felt different to the others and when I got my first job I can remember thinking, 'Oh great!'

She said she had no choice in the change of school and the reason for the move was because she was assessed as having 'high frequency deafness'. She also explained that the reason she got into trouble for her needlework was because:

I couldn't concentrate because I've got a lazy eye and I just couldn't seem to keep the neatness straight.

Fiona's sister Shona who attended an independent school in the city, was described as 'awf'y brainy', as if Fiona wished to retain a sense of herself as the norm and her sister as abnormally bright. Despite this, Fiona was clearly making an unfavourable comparison between herself and her sister:

Shona did OK, she was very good at school and she made some good friends at school and has kept in touch with some of them.

Other group participants described the reason for their having been placed in a special school in terms of some other trait rather than having an intellectual impairment. Michael, for instance, said that the reason he was placed in a special school was because of his violence and then described an escape from school:

I was a violent boy . . . I remember I was determined to get over the primary school wall . . . I got over the netting . . . and I jogged and ran home . . . I never went back . . . some kids got onto me.

As researchers who had brought the group together to explore their collective identity, we were unsure how to proceed. Given the negative connotations which the group attached to learning difficulties, we felt that we should not impose on the group an identity which they themselves were rejecting. At the same time, we were struck by the extent of the denial, silence and subterfuge surrounding intellectual impairment in which professionals and voluntary organisations were complicit. Throughout their education, training and social activity, these people were grouped together on the implicit understanding that they had certain common characteristics and required particular types of provision. However, the basis of their social grouping and the attributed social identity which flowed from it appeared not to have been discussed by parents and professionals with those whose lives it concerned. It appeared that intellectual impairment, far from being celebrated, was too shameful to be discussed openly even with those who were being consigned to this category. The contrasting experience of, for example, deaf people is evident. Although deafness may at times be associated with damaged social identity, deaf people themselves celebrate their culture, using this as the basis for opposing disabling barriers (Corker, 1997). It is now associated with a rich culture of its own and difficulties which deaf people encounter in participating in mainstream society are attributed to social and economic barriers rather than individually based deficits (Corker, 1997). There is evidence that although intellectual impairment is used to justify social segregation, its existence is denied by professionals who identify it and individuals who are thus labelled.

This denial of intellectual impairment is noted by Harris (1995). He refers to Gowans and Hulbert's (1983) review of studies measuring the self-concept of people with intellectual impairment, which confirms that they prefer not to identify with 'mentally handicapped' others. Oliver (1986), using a repertory grid technique to assess the self-concept of a girl with Down's Syndrome, found that she did not wish to identify with mentally handicapped others. Jahoda, Markova and Cattermole (1988) also reported that people with 'mild mental handicap' were likely to define themselves as essentially the same as other 'non-handicapped people' rather than essentially different. Their mothers, on the other hand, tended to see their sons and daughters as essentially different. Jahoda, Markova and Cattermole concluded from this that people with learning difficulties recognise the stigma attached to intellectual impairment and do not automatically internalise this sense of negative worth, rather rejecting the negative label. A problem with this, of course, is that rejecting intellectual impairment as part of one's subjectivity may leave an absence of identity rather than a positive sense of self. Harris points to tentative evidence that people with learning difficulties who participate in self-advocacy groups may have higher self-concepts than others. Given that the system of education, training and employment is premised on the segregation of people with intellectual impairment from others and the imposition of special status, it would appear that this is likely to produce spoiled identities. There is clearly a need for work which explores the uses of self-advocacy to develop a positive sense of self without disavowing central elements of identity. The refusal of the identity and label 'learning difficulties' has significant political implications. Although sharing the same or similar material locations, the people in the research group displayed little consciousness of these and how they might seek to alter them. It is to competing understandings of this material base to which we now turn.

### The material basis of social inclusion

Following European social theorists such as Beck (1992), it has been suggested that life chances and experiences may no longer be determined by an individual's relationship to the economic base, but rather to the individualised negotiation of risk. Beck concedes that risk is not randomly distributed and that western societies display 'an amazing stability' (1992, p. 91), with wealth protecting some people against life hazards and poverty exposing others to 'an abundance of risk'. Such theories have wide implications for disabled people including those with learning difficulties. In our project we wished to consider the extent to which intellectual impairment exposes people to an abundance of risk and whether disability has an effect independent of social class. At the level of social policy, there is a current focus on the centrality of employment to social inclusion. New Labour's Welfare to Work policy is firmly rooted in notions of the redemptive power of employment; those who cannot participate will have their basic needs met but will be excluded from civil society. Given these theoretical and policy concerns with the relationship between access to financial resources and social inclusion, we were curious to know how people with learning difficulties construed their situation.

The male members of the group were very clear that the development of social relationships was contingent on access to employment. Bruce, a man who was approaching retirement but had never had a job, felt the lack of employment keenly:

> You need money to take your girlfriend out . . . Women should have jobs as well so they can go to the dances and enjoy themselves.

The type of job people would do in order to be paid differed. Michael described with distaste a job at a leisure centre where he was meant to tidy up equipment but was also asked to clean the toilets. Bruce disagreed with him:

> I wouldnae mind cleaning the toilets. It saves you wandering the streets. I wouldnae mind doing a scaffy's [street sweeper's] job. The job's dirty but the money's clean!

There was also a recognition of the link between an independent household and an intimate relationship. Michael, a young man who had recently left school, rejected the type of independent living available to those ascribed special status:

> Michael: My mum, she wants me to go into a hostel. I don't like it. My mum
> thinks it might be a good idea and I don't want to.
> Heather: Have you been to look at a hostel?
> Michael: No. I don't want it. I just want to get married.
> Heather: What d'you think the hostel would be like?
> Michael: Very soor.
> Heather: Soor? What's that?
> Michael: One, you don't get help, two, you would be left in the lurch . . . I would
> prefer to get married . . . It's the best chance for me.

Michael perceives accurately that the type of independent living available in a hostel with other disabled people is different from that associated with the acquisition of one's own home in the context of the formation of adult social relationships. In the absence of this possibility, his preferred solution is to remain at home with his mother.

## CONCLUSION

We began this paper by considering the way in which the disability movement has successfully focused attention on the politics of doing research. Whereas some have maintained that the social model implies research directly controlled by disabled people, we point out the difficulties which might arise in relation to people with learning difficulties if this principle were to be enforced. In the context of our current research project, we aimed to include people with learning difficulties in aspects of the data collection but for a range of reasons our original plans were scaled down. This, of course, is not to suggest that involvement of people with learning difficulties in the research process must inevitably be limited; greater involvement in the formulation of the project from the outset might have produced stronger links between the main research project and the research group. Furthermore, the type of research demanded by the ESRC is not necessarily compatible with time-consuming work of building research relationships with people with learning difficulties.

Despite these limitations, the research group suggested important themes and provided a commentary on ideas emerging from preliminary data analysis. The researchers were pushed into clarifying their emerging theories by explaining them in a straightforward manner to group participants. For instance, we had to find direct ways of asking people about the identification and negotiation of risk and whether the barriers to full social participation they encountered were cultural or material in origin. Furthermore, we had to think through the contradictions of inviting people to discuss the barriers associated with intellectual impairment, when it was apparent that they did not see themselves as people with learning difficulties. It seemed to us that there was a need for the further development of the type of self-advocacy promoted by groups like People First, which sees learning difficulties as associated with barriers to understanding and communication in a world which places great store by intellectual and verbal dexterity, but at the same time acknowledges the wealth of ability and potential which people with learning difficulties nonetheless possess and is committed to dismantling the social and economic barriers they encounter.

Our awareness of the dangers of exploitation in research relationships made us question what was gained by those who participated in the research group. The fact that they attended for almost a year, making considerable efforts to be there, suggested that they saw it as an enjoyable and worthwhile experience, but also, less positively, that for many there were no more pressing demands on their time as would have been the case for most adults with work and family commitments. Despite the fact that their lack of social involvement was not of our making, nonetheless their desire for ongoing contact with the researchers underlined their vulnerability and marginalisation. This made it all the more important for us to address issues of accountability and we were guided by Booth and Booth's (1993) ideas of what accountability in research with people with learning difficulties may mean. Although our research was not formulated by people with learning difficulties, we felt compelled to ensure that, as far as this were possible, our work would be supportive of rather than damaging to the lives of those who participated in it. Whilst supporting attempts to involve disabled people in research, and acknowledging that we have much to learn about how best to do this, we ultimately believe that research should be judged on its rigor, its ability to make sense of diverse experience and its capacity to make suggestions about the conditions which might improve people's lives.

## ACKNOWLEDGEMENT

Work reported in this paper was undertaken as part of the project *The Meaning of the Learning Society for Adults with Learning Difficulties,* funded by the ESRC as part of its *Learning Society Programme.* We are grateful for this support.

## REFERENCES

Abberley, P. (1987) The concept of oppression and the development of a social theory of disability. *Disability, Handicap and Society,* Vol. 2, no. 1, pp. 5–19.

Barnes, C (1996) Disability and the myth of the independent researcher. *Disability and Society,* Vol. 11, no. 1, pp. 107–11.

Baron, S. R., Gilloran, A. and Schad, D. P. (1995a) Collaboration in a time of change: from subjects to collaborators. *Social Sciences in Health,* Vol. 1, no. 3, pp. 175–88.

Baron, S.R., Gilloran, A. and Schad, D. P. (1995b) Collaboration in a time of change: blocks to collaboration. *Social Sciences in Health,* Vol. 1, no. 4, pp. 195–205.

Beck, U. (1992) *Risk Society: Towards a New Modernity.* London: Sage.

Booth, T. and Booth, W. (1993) Accentuate the positive: a personal profile of a parent with learning difficulties. *Disability and Society,* Vol. 8, no. 4, pp. 377–92.

Clough, P. and Barton, L. (1995) Introduction: self and the research act, in P. Clough, and L. Barton (eds.) *Making Difficulties: Research and the Construction of Special Educational Needs.* London: Paul Chapman.

Corker, M. (1997) *Deaf and Disabled or Deafness Disabled.* Buckingham: Open University Press.

Crow, L. (1996) Including all our lives: renewing the social model of disability, in Barnes, C. and Mercer, G. (eds.) *Exploring the Divide: Illness and Disability.* Leeds: The Disability Press.

Duelli Klein, R. (1983) How to do what we want to do: the ethics and politics of interviewing women, in C. Bell and H. Roberts (eds.) *Social Researching: Politics, Problems, Practice.* London: Routledge and Kegan Paul.

Fraser, N. (1997) *Justice Interruptus: Critical Reflections on the Post-Socialist Condition.* London: Routledge.

French, S. and Swain, J. (1997) Changing disability research: participatory and emancipatory research with disabled people. *Physiotherapy* Vol. 83, no. 1, pp. 26–32.

Giddens, A. (1989) *Sociology* Cambridge: Polity.

Goode, W. J. and Hatt, P. K. (1952) *Methods in Social Research,* New York: McGraw Hill.

Gowans, F. and Hulbert, H. (1983) Self-concept assessment of mentally handicapped adults: a review. *British Institute of Mental Handicap* Vol. 11, pp. 121–3.

Harris, P. (1995) Who am I? Concepts of disability and their implications for people with learning difficulties. *Disability and Society,* Vol. 10, no. 3 pp. 341–53.

Jahoda, A., Markova, I. and Cattermole, M. (1988) Stigma and the self-concept of people with a mild mental handicap. *Journal of Mental Deficiency Research,* Vol. 32, pp. 103–15.

Mies, M. (1983) Towards a methodology for feminist research, in G. Bowles and R. Duelli Klein (eds.) *Theories of Women's Studies.* London: Routledge and Kegan Paul.

Minkes, J., Townsley, R. and Weston, C. (1995) Having a voice: involving people with learning difficulties in research. *British Journal of Learning Disabilities,* Vol. 25, pp. 77–80.

Morgan, D. (1981) Man, masculinity and the process of sociological enquiry, in H. Roberts (ed.) *Doing Feminist Research.* London: Routledge and Kegan Paul.

Oakley, A. (1981) Interviewing women: a contradiction in terms, in H. Roberts (ed.) *Doing Feminist Research.* London: Routledge and Kegan Paul.

Oliver, C. (1986) Self-concept assessment: a case study. *Mental Handicap,* Vol. 14, pp. 24–5.

Oliver, M. (1992) Changing the social relations of research production? *Disability, Handicap and Society.* Vol. 7, no. 2, pp. 101–14.

Phillips, A. (1997) From inequality to difference: a severe case of displacement? *New Left Review,* no. 224, pp. 143–53.

Riddell, S. Baron, S. and Stalker, K. (1995) The meaning of the learning society for adults with learning difficulties. Proposal to the Economic and Social Research Council, University of Stirling.

Scott, S (1984) The personable and the powerful: gender and status in sociological research, in C. Bell and H. Roberts. (eds.) *Social Researching: Politics, Problems, Practice.* London: Routledge and Kegan Paul.

Shakespeare, T. (1996) Rules of engagement: doing disability research. *Disability and Society,* Vol. 11, no. 1, pp. 115–21.

Shakespeare, T. and Watson, N. (1997) Defending the social model *Disability and Society.* Vol. 12, no. 2, pp. 293–301.

Stalker, K. (1997) Choices and voices: a case study of a self-advocacy group. *Health and Social Care in the Community.* Vol. 5, pp. 246–54.

Stalker, K. (1998) Some ethical and methodological issues in research with people with learning difficulties. *Disability and Society,* Vol. 13, no. 1, pp. 5–19.

Stanley, L. and Wise, S. (1983) *Breaking Out: Feminist Consciousness and Feminist Research.* London: Routledge and Kegan Paul.

Stronach, I. (1996) Fashioning post-modernism, finishing modernism: tales from the fitting room. *British Educational Research Journal,* Vol. 22, no. 3, pp. 359–77.

Townsley, R. (1995) Avon calling. *Community Care,* January, pp. 12–18.

Walmsley, J. (1994) Learning disability: overcoming the barriers? in S. French (ed.) *On Equal Terms: Working with Disabled People.* London: Butterworth Heinemann.

Whittaker, J., Gardner, S. and Kershaw, J. (1990) *Service Evaluation by People with Learning Difficulties.* London: The King's Fund Centre.

Young, I. M. (1990) *Justice and the Politics of Difference.* Princeton.

Zarb, G. (1992) On the road to Damascus: first steps towards changing the relations of research production. *Disability, Handicap and Society,* Vol. 7, no. 2, pp. 125–38.

# 8

# RESEARCHING ISSUES OF GENDER IN SPECIAL NEEDS EDUCATION

## Harry Daniels

### INTRODUCTION

In this chapter I will attempt to discuss the implications for research and the practice of teaching of the ways in which academic domains, policies and services are classified and organised. I will raise a number of issues that were considered in the course of a study[1] which sought to audit and analyse resource allocation practices at Key Stage 2 of the National Curriculum for 7–11-year-old children. In attempting to raise matters of authenticity and validity in interviews and document analysis I will also attempt to discuss the ways in which notions of voice, particularly with reference to disability and difficulty, are positioned.

### DIALOGUE

In *Making Difficulties* (Clough and Barton, 1995) Hazel Bines discussed ways of confronting personal and social constructs in research on special educational needs.

> The constructs held by individuals are likely to involve a mixture of political, ethical and theoretical ideas which have been shaped by particular knowledge, values and experience and by membership of particular social groups. (Bines, 1995, p. 43)

In her chapter Bines discusses some of the difficulties associated with the social formation of personal constructs of the world. This interplay between the social and the personal has, as Bines suggests, all too often been neglected in research contexts.

[1] ESRC Funded study R000235059 Gender and Special Educational Needs Provision in Mainstream Schooling, Harry Daniels, Valerie Hey, Diana Leonard and Marjorie Smith.

One of the most important messages of *Making Difficulties* was the plea for the development of greater understanding of the ways in which the practices and associated discourses of the social sciences and education position researchers and research subjects. This is all the more important when the potential for competition and conflict between discourses is amplified as is the case in the construction of SEN in research practice.

This interplay between personal motives and the outcomes of social/ professional activities is revealed by Fletcher-Campbell (1996) who draws on the findings of the Small Steps Survey. The intention of the Small Steps initiative was to support the development of means of providing alternative forms of accreditation and certification for school-leavers in the context of whole-school policies. The meaning that is attached to practices such as alternative forms of accreditation by pupils and the values of teachers who operate such systems are of crucial significance. As mere devices they will achieve little. They may even become threatening to the original intention.

The use of the concept of quality of life in the evaluation of the effects of special services and support has been proposed as a possible way of avoiding such unintended consequences. Decisions about whether someone should be given some particular form of provision such as to be 'integrated' may then be made in the context of the question as to whether 'being integrated' is likely to improve the quality of their life. This approach carries with it the implicit suggestion that global statements about desirable states of integration have, at times, lacked the validating voice of the client. The evaluation of services in terms of the quality of life of the client has been suggested as an alternative to monitoring **access** to services alone. Put bluntly, we still know far too little about the consequences of our actions.

The move to a 'quality of life' approach is not without its problems. There is little agreement as to the meaning of the term 'quality'. Pfeffer and Coote (1991) provide an overview which distinguishes between types of notions of quality (see Figure 8.1).

The **traditional approach** with its emphasis on perfection and high standards of production is far too expensive in these days of diminishing resources for welfare and support systems. The **scientific approach** with its emphasis on fitness for purpose provides the suggestion that measurement of the extent to which welfare services result in equal chances is a way forward. The **managerial approach** with its, now familiar, emphasis on excellence, notional customer satisfaction and contractual agreements about services gives support for the practice of listening and responding flexibly to diverse and changing needs. The **consumerist approach** attends to a crucial factor which is not usually associated with other approaches. It brings the notion of empowerment as a means and an end into the debate. If learners with disabilities and difficulties are to be given an active role with enforceable rights then means must be sought to enable them to engage.

We need an operational definition of the term quality which draws from the

## Approaches to Quality

| Type | Features | Problems | Uses |
|---|---|---|---|
| Traditional | Perfection High standards of production | Cost | |
| Scientific | Fitness for purpose | Professional power | Measuring equal chance |
| Managerial | Excellence Customer satisfaction Contracts | Managerial power Powerless consumers | To listen and respond flexibly to diverse and changing needs |
| Consumerist | Active role for the consumer Enforceable individual rights | Fails to distinguish between commerce and welfare | Empowerment as a means and an end |

After Pfeffer, N. and Coote, A. (1991)        *Is Quality Good for You?*        London: IPPR

**Figure 8.1**   Approaches to quality

strengths of these approaches and that will be of value to service providers and clients. If we are to suggest that learners have a right to education that improves their quality of life then we need to reach an agreement about the processes through which we negotiate the meaning of quality with and for individuals.

There are those pedagogies in which control over the sequencing, pacing and criteria of evaluation rest with the teacher. Practices (or indeed any kind of service) of this kind usually involve the prescription of content and method by the teacher. The assumption is made that the service provider/teacher knows, or can easily find out, what a client/learner needs. The set of possibilities for service provision/teaching is defined in advance and the job of the service provider/teacher is to allocate the learner/client to the 'appropriate' position. This may happen in the context of a curriculum-based assessment with a fixed curriculum script as well as in general resource allocation practices. If we accept a model of active construction in learning then we need appropriate forms of pedagogic practice. There seem to me to be at least two basic requirements for such practice. Firstly, it should be designed to allow for pedagogic dialogue between teacher and learner. Secondly, it should be designed to help the learner attain a 'voice' in such dialogue and thus to make a contribution to decision-making processes. These should be systems that empower learners and facilitate the development of independent (although not always individual) learning.

In our work we are faced with at least two levels of concern. In schools we are concerned with the position of learners who are not included in the processes which lead to the formulation of their special provision. We are also concerned with the various perspectives within school life and culture that may remain closed from each other. Thus within schools pupils' voices may not be heard and groups of professional concern may not 'hear' each other. In academic life, we are concerned that the discourses of disability, gender and race tend to remain insulated from one another. Along with many others we remain concerned that research is 'done' on people with disabilities not with or by them (Clough and Barton, 1995).

## THE CONCEPT OF 'VOICE'

The term 'voice' is central to our concern for the ongoing development of an account of the social formation of mind (cf. Cole, Engestom and Vasquez, 1997). Of the many common points to be found in the work of Vygotsky (1978, 1987) and Bakhtin (1986) there are three which are of particular relevance to the concept of voice. Firstly, they shared an assumption that to understand the mental action that is human consciousness it is necessary to understand the way in which semiotic devices, such as words and visual images, mediate such action. They also argue for the centrality of communicative practice in the formation of mind.

> The use of the term voice provides a constant reminder that even psychological processes carried out by an individual in isolation are viewed as involving processes of a communicative nature. (Wertsch, 1991, p. 13)

Perhaps most importantly they insist that individual mental activity has its origins in social activity and communication and that it is dialogue which characterises such events. Wertsch (1991) provides an eloquent summary of the overall implication of this position.

> The Bakhtinian focus on dialogicality presupposes more than one voice. In addition the notion of heterogeneity in thinking contrasts with the assumption, often implicit and often ethnocentric, that there is only one way, or that there is an obvious best way, to represent the events and objects in a situation. The notion of heterogeneity calls on us to consider why certain forms of speaking and thinking (voices) rather than others are invoked on particular occasions. It also forces us to recognise that we cannot answer this question simply on the basis of the metaphor of possession . . . of concepts and skills. Instead, we must consider how and why a particular voice . . . is privileged in a particular setting. (Wertsch, 1991, p. 14)

This approach leads us to question the way we communicate in research. The words we use, the grammatical devices we employ may be rightly seen (to paraphrase Bakhtin) as 'warm with the meanings of others'. Forms of speech and written text carry with them a socio-historical legacy. This is not to argue for some kind of anodyne, academic political correctness, rather it is to suggest that we should both seek to be aware of and understand the ways in which our personal research languages seek to construct subjects and mediate ideas.

There are multiple dimensions for the heterogeneity of voice within the project I am discussing here. We are a 'multidisciplinary team' comprised of three women and one man. Our academic roots lie in psychology, sociology and anthropology, feminist theory and education. We work in different settings. At the time when the project started one of us worked in a school as a SENCO, another was employed in a social science research unit, a third directed a centre for research and education on gender and the fourth was working in a department of educational psychology and special educational needs. In *Making Difficulties* it was suggested that we each come to research projects with our own assumptions about SEN/Disability and with our own specific questions and research agendas (Clough and Barton, 1995, p. 3). We recognise this in our own work. We each bring our own values based on our particular experiences of academic, personal and professional life. The standpoints we have assumed and acquired are to some extent reflections of our own self-identity. These identities are to some extent conditioned by matters of class, gender and age.

In order to engage in a common research activity we had to negotiate the means by which these 'within group' differences would be brought to bear on an agreed set of questions. Rather than trying to achieve consensus we sought a means by which tensions and differences could be brought into productive interplay. The unspoken element of this attempt at creative dialectic is, of course, hierarchy. Universities create and maintain vertical and horizontal patterns of power. Some departments are more powerful than others. Particular titles and positions are associated with the ability to access and wield political and academic influence. Thus questions of power and competition between discourses must be addressed.

## BOUNDARIES AND SEPARATIONS

The boundaries that exist in the social organisation of academic life are also reflected in the texts that have been produced in our area of research. An initial literature search revealed a dearth of research in which attempts had been made to bring the perspective of gender to bear on matters of concern within special needs education. Arguably, the assumptions of linearity and additivity implicit in some statistical models have been realised in the research activity itself. The assumptions of analysis of variance do not hold when cast against the complexity of the interweaving of factors such as race, gender, class and disability.

Most of the data from the positivist tradition concerning gender ratios in special provision relate to segregated special schooling. There are some data from the USA that suggest an over-referral of males, especially African Americans (Haigh and Malever, 1993–1994; Weinstein, 1993–1994). At the same time, the National Longitudinal Transition Study of Special Education Students (NLTS) reports that while girls are under-represented, those certified are more seriously impaired:

> Females in secondary special education represented a different combination of abilities and disabilities than males. As a group, females were more seriously impaired; even among males and females with the same disability category, females had marginally greater functional deficits than males. (Wagner, 1992, pp. 33–4)

We also know that there has been marked disparity of provision for boys and girls in access to many special schools in the UK. This has recently been confirmed by large-scale surveys (Cooper, Upton and Smith, 1991). OFSTED (1996a, 1996b) have also noted disparities by race and gender in school attainment.

The post-structuralist work of Henriques *et al.* (1984), Walkerdine (1981, 1985) and Connell (1995) signals the significance of discourses in the construction and negotiation of social subjectivities, and analytic attention is paid to the role of language in the production of subjectivity. Such work has emphasised the density and variability of 'how we come to be who we are'. Our work seeks to establish how educationalists come to conceive of children as particular sorts of learners in specific learning/schooling settings. More specifically we ask what are the gendered (raced and classed) differences in play in how pupils mediate teachers' as well as each others' social and educational roles/practices in the context of their interpersonal worlds.

Recent work on classrooms stresses the importance of recognising the complex nature of the relations that exist between different pedagogic messages, practices and subjects' social positioning (Reay, 1991). Debates about the **ineffectiveness** of previous pedagogic or equality initiatives have raised important questions about how different pupils read such intentions (Davies, 1989; Jones, 1993; Kenway and Blackmore, 1995).


## THE GENDER AND SPECIAL NEEDS RESEARCH PROJECT (GENSEN)

Our project was concerned with the gender differences in special needs practices in mainstream schools. As we noted in Daniels *et al.* (1995), it grew out of a pilot study which involved an audit of all forms of SEN support in mainstream primary schools. The pilot study schools were selected on the basis of LEA officer perceptions of high levels of commitment to equal opportunities policy and practice. The general pilot project findings were that:

● Significant gender differences exist in numbers of children receiving extra support irrespective of the identification procedure (teacher-based assessment or normative test-based screening).

- The effective reasons for referral reveal gender differences. These reasons are rarely made explicit if referral is made to agencies outside the school or, in some cases, outside the classroom.

- Boys are often given forms of support which are not designed to meet the needs identified.

When we reported back the data we had collected to the staff in the LEAs and schools concerned, they were alarmed, even shocked. Teachers often realised that more boys than girls were being given special help, but even those sensitive to the issue through involvement in equal opportunities work underestimated the extent to which this was occurring. It appeared that the perspectives on SEN practice in the schools were highly individualised. The accounts we collected from teachers about placement in SEN provision were quite distinct from more general accounts of social processes in schooling. We heard nothing of bias by gender and race in special provision whereas there was considerable energy devoted to such matters in the main body of the schools. It was as if the shift into special provision was associated with a shift in the accounts of causation given by teachers. In real terms this meant that equal opportunities monitoring procedures did not extend to special provision and practice within the schools.

As we argued in Daniels *et al.* (1995), if we focus not only on **who** gets special educational provision, but also on **how and why**, we need to look both at national, local and institutional (school) policies and provision, and at the social processes through which children come to be identified as having special needs, understand themselves to have 'special needs', and receive (or do not receive) available provision – as well as at how all such policies and processes are gendered. However, we are a long way from being able to provide such a full account, largely because explanations in the three areas involved – the nature of special educational provision, the conceptualisation of special educational needs, and analyses of gender inequalities – each have their specific foci and are the concern of different academic disciplines (and hence use different language and concepts/discourses); and because these different sorts of explanation have, up to now, been assiduously kept apart. In our own work we are attempting to connect such explanations.

The impact of different language and concepts/discourses became all too apparent when we came to collect information in schools. In this first phase of the project we experienced a number of difficulties collecting data. We found many examples of headteachers having access to information which was not available to Special Needs Co-ordinators (SENCOs). We also found that descriptors applied to children and services were used in an inconsistent manner across the LEA. There was evidence of idiosyncratic use of services across schools and large differences in levels of statementing. Despite the use of agreed frameworks and procedures, we ourselves differed in the way we placed priority on particular forms of data. The level of probing conducted in each interview could be seen to reflect personal priorities and preoccupations. These differences seemed to bear little relation to the nature of the school population. The LEA in which the study took place used a set of indicators, including eligibility for free school meals, to allocate the additional educational needs budget (AEN) to schools. The average gender ratio across schools for children with non-statemented special educational needs was 2:6. (All these figures were adjusted for the total numbers of boys and girls in each school.) In another very similar LEA authority which uses an audit with explicit criteria to allocate the AEN the average gender ratio was 2:4. These data suggest that an audit may not do much to alter the overall gender ratio. However, we noted that the variation between schools was much less in the LEA which used an audit. The use of objective criteria for the allocation of resources may seek to curb excessive over-representation of boys in non-statemented special needs provision.

Categories may be thought of as relays of social priorities and assumptions in the way that they enter the practices and discourses of resource allocation and management. For example, it is clear that monitoring systems, such as LEA SEN audits of need, account for some groups and not others. In the two LEAs we considered in our own work, gender and race were not monitored. Difficulties in monitoring are compounded by general difficulty in collating systems of records within and between schools. In several schools we found that there were several different sources of information about pupils with SEN. These were maintained by different teachers, support staff or groups of teachers. For example, it was not unusual to find three sources in one school: the headteacher, the SENCO and the school secretary. These datasets were overlapping but not identical. For example, the same pupil would be recorded as having different needs in two sources; and some children would be included in some lists and not others. In one case we were given a list of external support services with which pupils were placed only to discover that the LEA had withdrawn the service some three years ago.

Many of the terms in popular use have highly situated meanings. The variation between and within LEAs in the use of terms may, in part, be seen to depend on the quality and nature of the provision available within mainstream schools. In addition, resource allocation devices may generate categories into which data are forced. For example, if there is a large service which offers support for the development of reading it may be that children whose behaviour causes their teachers concern are 'redescribed' as needing help with their reading. We may only speculate as to whether this actually results in the manipulation of perceptions into administrative categories. Certainly there are complex relations between the language of description, with its categories and criteria, the administrative procedures and practices and the pedagogic reality. The very complexity and obscurity of these systems may allow for the relative autonomy of local ideology.

One prompt to this suggestion was the finding that there was no association between the level of SEN activity and resource allocation and the Additional Educational Needs (AEN) budget for the schools we surveyed in one LEA.


## ACTIVITY THEORY

Our research team is comprised of individuals whose main activities rest in settings which are, to some large degree, bounded from each other. The academic practices in which we engage are mediated by and through specific discourses. In trying to carry our work forward we have struggled to develop a forum in which these competing discourses can come into productive interplay. Our research suggests that the practices of schools reveal similar patterns of dislocation and insulation. One attempt at coming to understand these phenomena is to locate our analysis within the activity theory framework that has developed from the work of L. S. Vygotsky. It may be that this perspective opens a way to greater understanding of the processes of social formation which inhabit research practice. What follows is an attempt to provide a theoretical position which can be used to understand the ways in which multi-disciplinary research and professional practice proceed and to provide a language with which to intervene.

Vygotskian theory argues for the analysis of problem-solving as culturally and historically situated. That is, we need to understand the ways in which a particular problem-solving activity is embedded in a set of cultural practices and institutions at a specific point in their historical evolution. Thus the physical and institutional context of an activity, the social roles and status of the individuals involved, the cultural mediators available, and the prevalent cultural values and beliefs about the activity support and constrain the participants' attitudes, goals, understandings and actions (after Minick, Stone and Forman, 1993). This applies as much in the context of interdepartmental study in a university as it does in multiprofessional practice in schools.

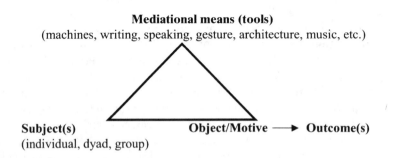

**Mediational means (tools)**
(machines, writing, speaking, gesture, architecture, music, etc.)

**Subject(s)**                    **Object/Motive** ⟶ **Outcome(s)**
(individual, dyad, group)

**Figure 8.2**   An activity system (fundamental unit of analysis of social practices)

Activity theory developed from the original Vygotskian thesis. It advocates the use of the activity system (see Figure 8.2) as the basic unit of analysis of behaviour, individual and collective (Leont'ev, 1981). In Vygotsky's account of the social formation of mind he was particularly concerned with the mediational properties of tools and signs, most notably speech. Speech, acting as a psychological tool, was seen to act as a mediator between the individual and the social world. It was not the vehicle of social determinism, rather it was theorised as one of many possible reflexive tools. This theoretical position draws attention to the way in which researchers and practitioners talk to each other. The tools of speech that professional communities use seek to both determine and construct professional boundaries.

Activity systems are associated with what Bakhtin called 'social languages'. Rather than a model of single activity systems and single languages, it is a model that envisages a range of systems which interact. Each system will have its own directions and priorities. This is the basis for dialectical contradictions that arise within the complexities of activity settings. Individuals are subject to multiple influences and the priorities of multiple agendas. Bakhtin's (1986) notion of heteroglossic voices is seen as the evidence of such forces in a classroom or in any other setting. These contradictions are the driving force of the development of systems. They are also crucial to understanding the dynamics of voice in both individual and group behaviour. The resolution, or partial resolution, of these contradictions will witness the emergence of a leading activity; the activity that ultimately motivates the system. Thus the study of development within activity theory requires an analysis of power and control in order to trace the genesis of voice. The textbooks, research reviews, laboratory apparatus and written procedures, lectures, conferences, and so on we will call 'classroom genres' – genres that develop in educational activity systems to operationalise teaching and learning (and selection) (Christie, 1993). Within a university or comprehensive secondary school, there are myriad classroom genres, in many media. These genres operationalise the more or less (but never entirely) routine interactions – what Bourdieu (1990) calls the habitus – among students' activity systems (families, peer groups, etc.) and the activity systems of disciplines: written genres such as dissertations, theses, research papers, essays, book reports, précis, lab reports, and so on (not to mention oral, gestural, architectural and other genres) (after Russell, 1997).

Such settings make very specific demands on individuals.

Each person entering the discursive complexes of a scientific field must learn to cope with those communicative means and processes that mediate participation with others. From a Vygotskian perspective, the mediating communicative patterns are tools for action and cognition. Though each participant in a discursive field need not think alike – indeed the discursive activities of disciplines largely rely on people not thinking precisely alike – each must draw on a common body of resources, cope with the same body of material and symbolic artifacts, master the same tools, and gain legitimacy for any new resources they want to bring into the

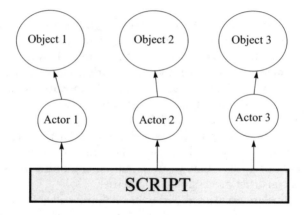

**Figure 8.3**   The general structure of co-ordination

field by addressing the same mechanisms of evaluation by which new concepts, tools or phenomena gain standing in the discourse. (Bazerman, 1997, p. 305)

In our own work we have become all too aware of such matters. As each researcher has developed and refined their understanding of the other discourses in play within the project, so they have also become aware of the limited nature of that understanding. The subtleties and nuances of forms of reference and analysis constitute major areas of potential misunderstanding. Our work has taken place in a context where we all realised that such phenomena would be in play. We had undertaken to focus directly on such matters. In much of the, supposedly, multiprofessional practice that takes place in schools there is not even this commitment to understanding and resolving conceptual and communicative difficulties. Indeed the boundaries that serve to constitute barriers to communication may also be seen to act as relays of professional power struggles.

In order to try and discuss innovation and improvement of specific forms of multiprofessional activity, Engestrom *et al.* (1997) develop a three-level notion of the developmental forms of epistemological subject–object–subject relations.

They call these three levels 'co-ordination, co-operation and communication'. Within the general structure of co-ordination, actors follow their scripted roles pursuing different goals (see Figure 8.3). Within this general structure of co-ordination it is possible to describe some of the research activity concerned with gender and special needs education. Researchers from different disciplines speak with their distinctive voices, each to their own agenda. The result is research which is internally fractured and potentially incoherent. It is equally possible to describe the workings of 'multidisciplinary teams' in the same way. The end result of both research and professional practice is almost inevitably the exclusion of the client/pupil/patient from the formulation of what counts as 'quality'.

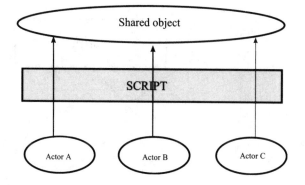

**Figure 8.4** The general structure of co-operation

Within the general structure of co-operation, actors focus on a shared problem. Within the confines of a script the actors attempt to both conceptualise and solve problems in ways which are negotiated and agreed (see Figure 8.4). The script itself is not questioned. That is the tacitly assumed traditions and/or the given official rules of engagement with the problem are not challenged.

Rogers and Whetton (1982) define and compare co-operation and co-ordination as follows:

- **Co-operation** is defined as, 'deliberate relations between otherwise autonomous organisations for the joint accomplishments of individual goals'. This definition stresses more informal relations, autonomy and individual goals.
- By comparison, **co-ordination** is 'the process whereby two or more organisations create and/or use existing decision rules that have been established to deal collectively with their shared task environment'.

Eraut (1994) drew an important distinction between reflection 'in action' and reflection 'on action'. Whilst reflection in action may well occur in co-operative and co-ordinated systems, reflection on action is more difficult to attain. Engestrom *et al.* (1997, p. 373) discuss reflective communication 'in which the actors focus on reconceptualising their own organisation and interaction in relation to their shared objects and goals. This is reflection on action. Both the object and the script are reconceptualised, as is the interaction between the participants.'

In our research we have been attempting to construct a general structure of communication as outlined in Figure 8.5. The 'script' that we use to direct our joint research action is open to critical interrogation and development. This is not always comfortable. Professional and academic groups often develop codes or shorthand means of communication and negotiation. These are often based on assumptions of shared interpretation that in practice do not exist. It is often difficult to explain that which is tacit in communicative practice within professional or academic domains. When tacit assumptions are questioned from

*Articulating with Difficulty*

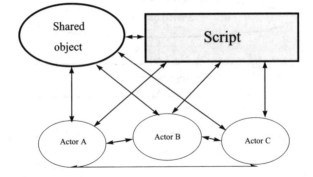

**Figure 8.5**   The general structure of communication

'outside', defensive behaviour often results, as is so often the case in multi-professional decision-making in settings such as those created within special needs systems.

Implicit in this general structure of communication is a version of Vygotsky's (1978) concept of the Zone of Proximal Development (ZPD). That is the 'area that is beyond one's full comprehension and mastery, but that one is still able to fruitfully engage with, with the support of some tools, concepts and prompts from others' (Bazerman, 1997, p. 305). The concept has also been used to consider the way in which peers prompt each other dialogically. The emphasis is on reciprocal support for mutual understanding. Newman, Griffin and Cole (1989, p. 136) describe this form of activity in the classroom:

> The multiple points of view within a ZPD are not seen as a problem for analysis but rather the basis for a process of appropriation in which children's understandings can play a role in the functional system.

Lave and Wenger (1991) distinguish between a 'scaffolding' and a 'collectivist' or 'societal' interpretation of the original formulation of the ZPD. The 'scaffolding' interpretation is one in which a distinction is made between support for the initial performance of tasks and subsequent performance without assistance:

> the distance between problem-solving abilities exhibited by a learner working alone and that learner's problem-solving abilities when assisted by or collaborating with more experienced people.

This definition could give rise to learning in classrooms, and activity in multi-professional teams and research teams, which resembles the co-ordination model outlined above. In the 'collectivist' or 'societal' perspective, they cite a definition of the ZPD as the 'distance between the everyday actions of individuals and the historically new form of the societal activity that can be collectively generated. Under such societal interpretations of the concept of the zone of proximal development, researchers tend to concentrate on processes of social transformation. This involves the study of learning beyond the context of pedagogical structuring, including the structure of the social world in the analysis, and taking into account the conflictual nature of social practice (after Lave and Wenger, 1991, pp. 48–9). This definition leads to activity as envisaged in the communication model.

This envisages activity systems that contain a variety of different viewpoints or 'voices', as well as layers of historically accumulated artifacts, rules and patterns of division of labour. This multivoiced and multilayered nature of activity systems is both a resource for collective achievement and a source of compartmentalisation and conflict. Contradictions are the engine of change and development in an activity system as well as a source of conflict and stress (Cole, Engestom and Vasquez, 1997, p. 4).

If the activity theory approach provides an appropriate means of conceptualising the research process and educational practices which concern us here, then it should also provide directions for the development of conceptual tools and methodological principles. Engestrom (1993) outlines three principles of activity theory:

- using a collective activity system as the unit of analysis
- searching for internal contradictions as the driving force behind disturbances, innovations and change in the activity system
- analysing the activity and its constituent components and actions historically.

This work has been applied with some success in a range of contexts (e.g. primary care medical practice, Engestrom (1993); and postal delivery services and law courts, Engestrom *et al.* (1997)). Research such as our own calls for the application of such principles.

As noted above, 'in trying to carry our work forward we have struggled to develop a forum in which these competing discourses can come into productive interplay' in order to reflect *on* our own research action. This is not always a comfortable process. If we follow Engestrom's (1993) suggestion, we need to understand the research process as an activity system. This calls for a deliberate focus on the way we talk and set about our work. The terms, concepts and methods which are introduced into the activity must be understood as much in terms of the socio-historical baggage which they bring with them as in terms of the, often implicit, assumptions from which they have arisen. Thus the focus of the research process must be on the 'scripts' and patterns and modes of communication as much as shared objects of activity. It is through this attention to 'scripts' and patterns of communication that the explicit and implicit contradictions will be revealed. Although it is sometimes difficult to remember that these contradictions should be seen as the driving force of our own work, this is of the utmost importance. The struggle to understand the differences that exist between academic traditions and professional orientations requires far more attention. This is not to suggest that all differences should be resolved and that there is some undifferentiated nirvana in which professional and

academic life would be perfect. We need to find ways in which differences can
be brought into productive interplay rather than denial or destructive conflict.
Professional boundaries and differences serve an important purpose. They
serve to create communities within which specialised activity and associated
discourse can be developed and refined. These communities exist to produce
powerful, specialised tools of enquiry. The application of these tools in the
complexity of everyday research and professional practice requires us to relin-
quish the vanities of our own subgroupings and seek to understand the contradictions that are revealed in and by our own perspectives in practice. This can
help us to develop our own specialism and also to engage in practices which
are genuinely multi-faceted. Tacit affiliation to consensus will not help us to
challenge the boundaries that **make difficulties** for so much multidisciplinary
work and research practice. Contradiction should not be seen as a professional
threat but as the future for development.


## REFERENCES

Bakhtin, M. (1986) *Speech Genres and Other Late Essays*. Edited by C. Emerson and
   M. Holquist. Austin: University of Texas Press.
Bazerman, C. (1997) Discursively structured activities. *Mind Culture and Activity*, Vol.
   4, no. 4, pp. 296–308.
Bines, H. (1995) Risk, routine and reward: confronting personal and social constructs
   in research on special educational needs, in P. Clough and L. Barton (eds.) *Making
   Difficulties: Research and the Construction of SEN*. London: Paul Chapman.
Bourdieu, P. (1990) *An Introduction to the Work of Pierre Bourdieu: the Practice of
   Theory*. Basingstoke, UK: Macmillan.
Christie, F. (1993). Curriculum genres: planning for effective teaching, in B. Cope and
   M. Kalantzis (eds.) *The Powers of Literacy: a Genre Approach to Teaching Writing*.
   London: Falmer Press.
Clough, P. and Barton, L. (eds.) (1995) *Making Difficulties: Research and the Con-
   struction of Special Educational Needs*. London: Paul Chapman.
Cole, M. C., Engestom, Y. and Vasquez, Olga (1997) Introduction, in *Mind, Culture
   and Activity*. Cambridge University Press.
Connell, R. W. (1995) *Masculinities*. Cambridge: Polity Press.
Cooper, P., Upton, G. and Smith, C. (1991) Ethnic minority and gender distribution
   among staff and pupils in facilities for pupils with emotional and behavioural diffi-
   culties in England and Wales. *British Journal of Sociology of Education*, Vol. 12, no.
   1.
Daniels, H., Hey, V., Leonard, D., and Smith, M. (1995) Gendered practice in special
   educational needs, in L. Dawtrey, J. Holland and M. Hammer (eds.) *Equality and
   Inequality in Education Policy*. Milton Keynes: Open University Press.
Daniels, H., Hey, V., Leonard, D. and Smith, M. (1996) Equal to the challenge. *Special*,
   Autumn.
Davies, B. (1989) *Frogs and Snails and Feminist Tails: Preschool Children and Gender*.
   Boston: Allen and Unwin.

Engestrom, Y. (1993) Developmental studies of work as testbench of activity theory: the case of primary medical practice, in S. Chaiklin and J. Lave (eds.) *Understanding Practice: Perspectives on Activity and Context*. Cambridge University Press.

Engestrom, Y., Brown, K., Christopher, L. C. and Gregory, J. (1997) Co-ordination, co-operation and communication in the courts: expansive transitions in legal work, in Cole, M. C., Engestom, Y. and Vasquez, Olga (eds.). *Mind, Culture and Activity*. Cambridge University Press.

Eraut, M. (1994) *Developing Professional Knowledge and Competence*. London: The Falmer Press.

Fletcher-Campbell, F. (1996) Just another piece of paper? Key Stage 4 accreditation for pupils with learning difficulties. *British Journal of Special Education*, Vol. 23, no. 1, pp. 15–19

Haigh, J. A., and Malever, M. G. (1993–1994). Special education referral practices by gender, ethnicity, and comparison to state and district enrollments. *CASE in Point*, 8 (1) pp. 13–24.

Henriques, J., Hollway, W., Urwin, C., Venn, C. and Walkerdine, V. (1984) *Changing the Subject: Psychology, Social Regulation and Subjectivity*. London: Routledge.

Jones, A. (1993) Becoming a 'girl': post-structuralist suggestions for educational research. *Gender and Education*, Vol. 5, no. 2, pp. 157–66.

Kenway, J. and Blackmore, J. (1995): Pleasure and pain: beyond feminist authoritarianism and therapy in the curriculum. Paper presented at the Unesco Colloquium 'Is there a Pedagogy for Girls?' Institute of Education, University of London, 10–12 January.

Lave, J. and Wenger, E. (1991) Practice, person and social world, in *Situated Learning: Legitimate Peripheral Participation*. Cambridge University Press.

Leont'ev, A. N. (1981). *Problems of the Development of Mind*. Moscow: Progress.

Minick, N., Stone, C. A., and Forman, E. A. (1993) Introduction: integration of individual, social and institutional processes in accounts of children's learning and development, in E. A. Forman, N. Minick and C. A. Stone (eds.) *Contexts for Learning: Sociocultural Dynamics in Children's Development*. Oxford University Press.

Newman, D., Griffin, P. and Cole, M. (1989) *The Construction Zone: Working for Cognitive Change in Schools*. Cambridge University Press.

Ofsted (1996a) *The Gender Divide: Performance Differences Between Boys and Girls*. London: HMSO.

Ofsted (1996b) *Recent Research on the Achievements of Ethnic Minority Pupils*, David Gillborn and Caroline Gipps. London: HMSO.

Pfeffer, N. and Coote, A. (1991) *Is Quality Good For You?* London: IPPR.

Reay, D. (1991) Intersections of gender, race and class in the primary school, *British Journal of Sociology of Education*, Vol. 12, no. 2, pp. 163–72.

Rogers, D. and Whetton, D. (1982) *Interorganizational Coordination: Theory, Research and Implementation*. Iowa: Iowa State University.

Russell, D. R. (1997) Rethinking genre in school and society: an activity theory analysis. *Written Communication*, Vol. 14, pp. 504 and 554.

Vygotsky, L. S. (1978) *Mind in Society: the Development of Higher Psychological Processes*. Cambridge, MA: Harvard University Press.

Vygotsky, L. S. (1987). Thinking and speech, in L. S. Vygotsky, *Collected Works* Vol. 1, pp. 39–285. R. Rieber and A. Carton (eds.) N. Minick. (trans.). New York: Plenum.

Wagner, M. (1992) Being female – a secondary disability? Gender differences in the transition experiences of young people with disabilities. Paper presented at the annual meeting of the American Educational Research Association, San Francisco, April.

Walkerdine, V. (1981) Sex, power and pedagogy. *Screen Education* Vol. 38, pp. 1–24.

Walkerdine, V. (1985) On the regulation of speaking and silence, in C. Steedman, C. Urwin and V. Walkerdine (eds.) *Language, Gender and Childhood*. London: Routledge and Kegan Paul.

Weinstein, D. F. (1993–1994). Special education referral and classification practices by gender, family status and terms used: a case study. *CASE in Point*, 8(1), pp. 25–36.

Wertsch, J. V. (1991) *Voices of the Mind*. London: Harvester.

# 9

# 'STORIES ABOUT WRITING STORIES': REAPPRAISING THE NOTION OF THE 'SPECIAL' INFORMANT WITH LEARNING DIFFICULTIES IN LIFE STORY RESEARCH

## *Dan Goodley*

### INTRODUCTION

The materialist doctrine that men *(sic)* are products of circumstances and upbringing, and that, therefore, changed men are products of other circumstances and changed upbringing, forgets that it is men who change circumstances and the educator must himself be educated. Hence this doctrine is bound to divide society into two parts, one of which is superior to society. The coincidence of the changing of circumstances and of human activity can be conceived and rationally understood only as revolutionising practice. (Marx, 1845, Theses on Feuerbach, in Marx and Engels, 1991, p. 28)

This chapter examines a piece of research that attempted to give a voice to the stories of self-advocates with learning difficulties. My experiences highlight a number of problems associated with 'giving voice' when assumptions of 'the disempowered' and 'the special' are used in preconceiving the actions of research participants. Eventually in my research a happy tale unfolded, with informants challenging my abstractions of 'special' through their own practical activity in the research context. In this chapter a research story is told to account for the stages of collaborative narrative inquiry that created the life stories of five self-advocates. In part one of the research story, a number of issues will be considered in relation to interviewing people with learning difficulties. Part two examines the writing of others' stories. Part three ends the research story with the tale of a research relationship that looks closer at the collaborative nature of life story research. The actions of each and every informant can be seen as revolutionising practice, which kept knocking me back into line when I strayed into actively 'making difficulties'.

## LIFE STORIES AND SELF-ADVOCACY

This chapter draws upon my PhD research that appraised self-advocacy in the lives of people with learning difficulties[1]. Part of the research aimed to give a voice to the experiences of people with learning difficulties who have had long-term involvement with self-advocacy groups. I understood 'giving voice' in this study as providing contexts for oppressed people to present their life experiences. Consequently five self-advocates, Jackie Downer, Lloyd Page, Joyce Kershaw, Anya Souza and 'Phillip Collymore' (a pseudonym) were interviewed. Together we presented their accounts in the form of life stories.

### Life as narrative

A current frame of reference in the social sciences is the epistemological notion that meaning and experience are constrained in texts (Parker and Shotter, 1990). Various approaches study texts to throw light on personal and social life. One of these is narrative inquiry (Clandinin and Connely, 1994). Narrative inquiry is concerned with the storied nature of life (Bruner, 1987). When a person notes something about their experience, they often do so in a storied form (Clandinin and Connely, 1994, p. 414). Some proponents of narrative inquiry assert that stories are *the* central component of experience and reality (Didion, 1979; Gergen and Gergen, 1988). Narrative is seen as producing experience, and vice versa. People story their lives to structure and give meaning. Indeed, people tell stories in order to live (Didion, 1979, p. 11). Alternatively, other proponents use narrative as a medium through which to present and reflect upon some of the experiences and realities of people (Allport, 1947; Parker, 1963; Plummer, 1983, 1995; Whittemore, Langness and Koegel, 1986). Here, reality and narrative are not necessarily seen as synonymous. Instead, storytelling is used as a method to lend some insight into the experiences and realities of narrators.

Narrative inquiry deals with the collection, writing up and presentation of stories (Plummer, 1983). Accounts of people with learning difficulties have taken a number of narrative forms including autobiography (Hunt, 1967), biography (Deacon, 1974), life story (Bogdan and Taylor, 1976), oral history (Angrosino, 1994) and life history (Whittemore, Langness and Koegel, 1986). This chapter focuses upon the collection of the life stories of five self-advocates.

### Life stories of self-advocacy

Life stories are life experiences presented in a storied form (Plummer, 1983). A life story is the product of the reminiscences of one narrator that are structured

---

[1] University of Sheffield, Department of Sociological Studies.

together chronologically or thematically in a storied fashion (Bertaux 1981). The life story relies on the accounts of a primary narrator whereas a life history combines different persons' stories of an individual (Plummer, 1983, 1995). Life stories can be written alone or told to others who collaborate in writing (Sparkes, 1994; Hatch and Wisnieswski, 1995). The aim of my research was to write life stories collaboratively with people with learning difficulties.

Life stories boast a number of strengths. First, inviting the life stories of people with learning difficulties into the research implies that their lives exist to be recounted and addresses the absence of these accounts in previous documents (Korbin, 1986, p. 19; Thompson, 1988, p. 2). Second, life stories address the 'disappearing individual' in abstract social theory (Whittemore, Langness and Koegel, 1986). Third, stories investigate some of the meanings held by narrators, and also by readers (Bogdan and Taylor, 1976; Smith, 1990). Finally, because writing stories is a reflexive venture, as a research exercise it can be reflected upon and investigated (Plummer, 1983). Some writers, like Parker (1963), assert that the very exercise of writing someone else's story can expose the non-scientific and arbitrary nature of research.

## The life story and making difficulties and differences

A recent paper has made a case for the use of narrative methods with people with learning difficulties (Goodley, 1996). In this chapter I want to take a critical look at my use of the life story method. As *Making Difficulties* outlined (Clough and Barton, 1995), in trying to give a voice to disempowered groups there is a danger that researchers re-emphasise passive and incomplete understandings of such groups. Clough and Barton ask a number of pertinent questions about researchers doing disability research (p. 3). One question stands out as particularly appropriate in view of my use of the life story method:

> What assumptions about SEN/disability do I have which are inevitably present in the way I conceive of the study?

John Swain's contribution (Chapter 6 of *Making Difficulties*), a critical reflection on the use of 'participatory research' with people labelled as having 'special educational needs', put forward a strong case for research *with* rather than *on* people. Swain concluded:

> If research is not constructed through participation it will confirm rather than challenge existing social constructions of special educational needs. (p. 92).

My research highlights the problems in doing research on people with learning difficulties. Specifically, difficulties were made when I took (able-bodied) abstractions of the perceived (in)activities of informants into the research context. Nevertheless following Clough and Barton's (1995, pp. 145–6) argument for the 'researcher as learner', my life story research highlights how narrators are more than able to redress oppressive assumptions and practices through their own activities. In spite of my making difficulties – unquestionably bringing into the research the notion of 'special' – informants became the key participants in a reassessment of the assumptions that underpinned my research. Eventually they educated someone who was acting like the educator.

## PART 1 OF THE STORY: INTERVIEWING TOP 'SELF-ADVOCATES'

To the layman, the chief fault with psychological science seems to be its willingness to pile abstraction upon abstraction with little regard for the concrete personal life. (Allport, 1947, p. 143)

### Access

Access was negotiated with reference to an introductory booklet that combined prose and pictures. Following Barnes (1994) and Walmsley (1995), the booklet introduced the research/er; explained how informants were contributing to the writing of a thesis and what would happen to participants' disclosures (life stories in thesis and published papers). Also explored was what both parties would get out of the research (submission of thesis for a PhD, copies of life stories for informants and hopes for publication of a self-advocate friendly report).

Research relationships are social relationships (Parker, 1963; Sparkes, 1994; Bannister *et al.*, 1994). Inequalities structured around gender, race, sexuality and disability enter the research context. Disclosing my involvement as a volunteer to a self-advocacy group appeared to encourage acceptance. As Anya Souza put it, she 'didn't mind my sort'. Also discussed was confidentiality (only I would see the transcripts) and the need to preserve the anonymity of others (because they had not been asked). Initially, all five were proud to have their names attached to their life stories. Later, 'Phillip Collymore' was to choose this pseudonym.

### General style of interviewing and 'telling stories'

Informants were asked for their 'life stories'. Anecdotes were presented chronologically, thematically and interspersed with opinions. Asking for stories, rather than experiences, may have invited expression (Reason and Hawkins, 1988, p. 100). Interviews varied in length from about an hour through to five hours. Total contact time was longer. Interviews were carried out in a variety of places, at home, in restaurants and cafés, and in a self-advocacy group's office.

Lofland (1971) asserts that the format and content of interviews should at all times follow the issues of significance identified by informants. In contrast, Tremblay (1959) argues that interviewers have interests that they will want to explore in the interview. I had some questions to ask but they were used mainly as reminders and were not needed as central themes around which to organise dialogue. All informants spoke openly, gave extended anecdotes, reflected on the experiences and considered present situations. Interviews consisted of a friendly and informal atmosphere and a conversational format. Informants did not just tell stories. Their reflections on past and present experiences were tangled up in opinions, views and attitudes.

### Over-enthusiastic interviewing

For Taylor and Bogdan (1984, pp. 77 and 94–6) the interviewer, not the interview protocol, is the research tool. Interviewers should continuously appraise the interview situation by opposing sterility, being non-judgemental, letting people talk and sensitively probing. Lloyd Page was the first to be interviewed and became the unfortunate recipient of over-enthusiastic questioning. Lowe and de Paiva (1988) have highlighted the 'tendency' for informants with learning difficulties to reply with simple yes or no answers. Atkinson (1993) found that frequently asked questions emphasised the researcher's interests and helped to build up trust and rapport. Flynn (1986) and Flynn and Saleem (1986) used direct questions to ascertain the views of people with learning difficulties. Perhaps such advice was taken too literally into the interview with Lloyd. I was impatient, fired quick questions and gave him little time to respond. He said afterwards that he felt 'grilled like a tomato'. Field notes, written after the interview, reflect on my failings:

> Some of the literature suggests snappy, quick questions 'work best' and perhaps I had gone into the interview with such preconceptions. This assumes all interviewees with learning difficulties are the same – they're not!

In contrast to Shakespeare (1993), who felt that she had acted too naturally in her interviews, Lloyd's interview highlighted problems with literature-based research posturing. Viewing Lloyd as a person with learning difficulties, who would respond best to a particular type of questioning, assumes that people with learning difficulties are a homogenous group and unquestionably translates 'textbook' guidelines into the research context (see Lawthom, 1996). Good informants are rarely found, rather they emerge in the course of one's everyday activities, not in artificially contrived research contexts (Taylor and Bogdan, 1984, p. 86; Edgerton, 1984).

### The pros and cons of 'natural' interviews

The four informants interviewed after Lloyd were approached in a more 'natural' way. I tried to strike up conversations in the same way that I would with peers when I really want to hear their opinions(!). Consequently, interview transcriptions revealed many leading questions. Some literature that deals with drawing information from people with learning difficulties suggests that leading questions are inappropriate. The reasoning behind this claim is the reported tendency of people so-labelled to respond affirmatively to questions regardless of their content (Sigelman *et al.*, 1980; Sigelman *et al.*, 1981; Sigelman *et al.*, 1982; also for general points see Orne, 1962).

Simons (1994) and Booth and Booth (1994) argue that assuming acquiescence, on the part of people with learning difficulties, unquestionably presumes deficit. Leading questions or 'probing' are a necessary part of the exchange of information between two people (Taylor and Bogdan, 1984, p. 98). In this sense, acting as 'naturally' as possible in interviews is a condition under which people come to know each other. The better the chat, the more leading the questions (Tremblay, 1959). Furthermore, the five informants in this study did not simply acquiesce. Joyce Kershaw ignored or spoke over some of my queries. Anya Souza presented long anecdotes that kept questions to a minimum. 'Phillip Collymore' queried questions, 'Say that again', and asked me to say a word that he couldn't, 'Vulnerable? That's right, that's the word.' Lloyd Page had obviously got sick of my grilling and played a videotape instead.

Anecdotes and opinions were responded to in a value-laden way. Hopefully, this made clear my interest in what informants had to say (see Atkinson, 1993). When people acquiesce, perhaps this is because they feel powerless. Maybe the informants in this study felt in control: a testimony to their involvement in self-advocacy. Nevertheless, acting naturally has implications. Informants' words were often reactions to my leading questions and value-laden responses. These 'natural exchanges' were used in constructing narrative. Consequently, my words may have unnecessarily littered the interview material that was later used for writing stories. With hindsight I could have balanced reacting to disclosures with keeping my opinions to myself.

### Reflecting on part 1 of the research story

I initially went into the interview with Lloyd Page assuming that he, and 'others like him', would be vulnerable and that interviews would be problematic. Lloyd helped me to reappraise these assumptions but perhaps I acted too naturally in subsequent interviews. The next section presents narrators challenging 'making difficulties' in the collaborative writing up of their life stories.

## PART 2 OF THE STORY: COLLABORATIVE NARRATIVE INQUIRY CHALLENGING ASSUMPTIONS OF 'SPECIAL'

If we wish to hear respondents' stories then we must invite them into our work, as collaborators, sharing control with them, so that together we try to understand what their stories are about. (Mischler, 1986, p. 249)

Little has been written about the writing of life stories (Plummer, 1983; Hatch and Wisniewski, 1995). In collaborative life story research the final draft of a life story is the narrative of both narrator and writer (Ferguson, Ferguson and Taylor, 1992, p. 299). Plummer (1983, p. 111) encourages life story researchers to:

> get your subject's words, come to really grasp them from the inside and then turn it yourself into a structured and coherent statement that uses the subject's words in places and the social scientist's in others but does not lose their *authentic* meaning. [my italics]

Two questions can be posed to explore the position of narrator and writer in collaborative narrative inquiry. First, how does the writer construct the life story of the narrator? Second, to what extent do narrators become involved in the writing of their own life story? The first question resonates with Dexter's (1956, p. 10) demands for 'a sociology of those who study mental deficiency'. As Atkinson (1993, p. 58) notes:

> There is, however, more to telling – and hearing – people's accounts of their lives and experiences than simply providing a forum. The role of the researcher, or listener, has a bearing on how stories unfold and what they are about.

Researchers have spent little time examining how they move from what they collect (e.g. interview transcripts) to what they tell (e.g. stories) (Plummer, 1983). More time is spent considering how information is collected (Walker, 1981, p. 157). Therefore, examining the hand of the researcher in the writing of stories would appear to constitute a useful exercise.

The second question takes on a particular slant in the case of life stories which are the creation of two minds working together (Whittemore, Langness and Koegel, 1986, p. 6). Bertaux-Wiame (1981, p. 264) argues that social investigation is not a matter reserved for researchers. Accordingly, the five informants responded to the opportunities presented in ways that illuminate notions of informant participation and empowerment.

### Step 1: writing the first drafts – 'special material' from 'special' relationships?

I was committed to representing the experiences of informants as fully and truthfully as possible. Unfortunately, I sometimes failed to see such commitments in my informants. Lloyd Page's mother was present at the interview. Justification for including her words in Lloyd's narrative can be based on the obvious impact that she has had on his life. As Lloyd put it, 'My mother has been great, she's never stopped me.' However, I was anxious that including Lloyd's mother's words was attaching greater authority to the words of another without learning difficulties. This passes over the dynamics of our meeting when Lloyd's mother actually stayed primarily in the background when he was talking. Again I was treating Lloyd as different, a 'special case' to the research norm. Interviews involving two or more people will undoubtedly result in discussion, disagreement, reflection and consultation and these should be seen as strengths. People tell the 'same story' in different ways (Bertaux-Wiame, 1981, pp. 259–60) making for a far more in-depth account. Who the storytellers are, however, is best to be acknowledged in the writing of narrative.

### Step 2: writing the second and final drafts – a collaborative venture and active informants

Informants were sent drafts of their life stories. They all made changes: reassessing the structure of their narratives, suggesting that paragraphs be moved and/or taken out, tenses changed from present to past, inverted commas added to convey a sense of critical usage of a word ('respite care' and 'bereavement') and corrections made. Narrators became far removed from 'special informant' status when contributing to the writing of their accounts. At first, narrators disclosed experiences to a writer who became the storyteller. Then, when the first drafts were given back, narrators addressed how their experiences appeared as stories in the written texts. The life story method appears to make links with Lather's (1991) 'fundamental point' about empowering research: the promotion of self-reflection and deeper understanding of the research situation by the research subjects. Informants participated in the formal presentation of their experiences.

However, whether or not the five informants felt empowered by their involvement in the research is a difficult question to answer. Neither were their lives changed markedly by their involvement, nor were they consulted about the links made between their stories and wider issues in the analysis sections of my thesis. Perhaps collaborative life story research injects only one consideration into the empowering disability research paradigm. As Sparkes (1994, p. 180) puts it:

> There is a need for researchers to move beyond paternalistic notions of 'giving' voice, towards a view of life story as an expression of solidarity with those who share their stories in the hope of creating individual and societal change.

Actually getting people with hidden lives into the research context may be the first step of praxis-orientated research (Ferguson, Ferguson and Taylor, 1992, p. 299; Goodley, 1996). Tapping into the common experience of storytelling allows a useful starting-point, where storytellers already exist. While all informants took up the challenge of narrative inquiry, one informant challenged the collaborative aspect of the research. This research relationship is documented in detail below and takes further a critical agenda with respect to 'giving voice'.

### PART 3 OF THE RESEARCH STORY – 'GIVE US A SAY JOYCE!' THE TALE OF A RESEARCH RELATIONSHIP IN NARRATIVE INQUIRY

The research relationship formed with Joyce Kershaw shows how informants can take up the challenge of narrative inquiry themselves. Out of the five research relationships, most time was spent face to face with Joyce Kershaw. She was the only one with two stories in my thesis: one that I wrote (Danny's story) and another that she wrote (Joyce's story). As she put it:

> Do you know I'd been thinking about writing my story for years. It was you who made me do it – you got me so mad.

Stages involved in the writing of the two stories constitute stories in their own right.

## Writing my story of Joyce Kershaw's life

### The first attempt

Around the time of writing 'Danny's story' I was trying to write how Joyce spoke. For Joyce, in went phrases such as, 'Oh they were', and, 'Yer knows'. Keeping with this personable style, in came lots of, 'I says . . . and then he says . . .' and her accent was represented through the additions of 'cause', 'owt', 'summat', and so on. Writing was easy. Long passages of prose were cut from the transcript and pasted into the draft narrative. I thought I was letting Joyce speak to the reader as she had to me. Soon afterwards I phoned Joyce to tell her that I'd finished her life story, and of my attempts to write how she spoke and the necessary name changes. She said she'd have a look at it.

A week later Joyce phoned me at home. She was not happy with the story. She wanted to meet up again to review it. At our next meeting I read aloud what I had written. As I read she was reminded of what she had told me. At times she would start retelling a story. I would interrupt to read from the part of the narrative, to show that I had got her anecdotes down on paper. However, Joyce remained unhappy about my writing style and asked for the first draft to be rewritten. I thanked Joyce for spending so much time with me. 'That's all right, thank you for listening to me,' she replied, 'but when you're writing my story Danny – use your imagination.' Her advice could be read as, 'Treat my stories with the respect they deserve'.

### Back to the drawing board

Joyce had identified a number of problems with the first draft. My attempts to have her talking to the reader through the narrative had failed. 'It's difficult to read,' she told me, 'When you were asking me questions and I was answering them, I would say, 'Then he says and I says,' but that was then – we were talking. I didn't realise I spoke like that!' In the second draft 'owt' became 'anything', 'summat' became 'something', and so on. There were also a few occasions when Joyce felt that I had not quite conveyed the significance of some of her experiences. Over the next two weeks I rewrote the narrative and felt rather pleased with myself. Together Joyce and I had written what I considered to be an illuminating life story. We had shared responsibilities. Joyce had also strengthened my position as researcher and improved my writing. In reflecting on phenomenologically grounded research, Heshusius (1987, p. 43) acknowledges that:

> research is exceedingly demanding . . . it requires one [the researcher] to be deeply interested in the lives of the persons one wants to understand . . . This approach to research requires *investment of oneself.* [my italics]

In addition, informants themselves have a vested interest in the presentation of their own stories. Left at this stage of the writing process, I believed that I had reason to view the research relationship as relatively collaborative, perhaps even empowering. Joyce and I had developed a similar research relationship to the one Sparkes (1994, p. 170) had with an informant:

> what might have been defined as an impediment (our differences) in terms of the development of collaboration has been used as a resource to enrich the collaborative nature of the interaction.

The story did not stop there with Joyce Kershaw. There was a further twist in the research tale.

## Joyce writes her own story

### Rejecting collaboration

I had posted the second draft to Joyce some days before we met up in a local café. As Joyce came in from the cold, she greeted me with a whack around the head from her scarf. 'I'm fed up with you,' she said with a glint in her eye. 'I thought blow it – I'll write me bloody own.' She produced my story from her handbag, and placed it on the table. I turned over the bound sheets and saw that she had handwritten her own story on the back. 'There's twelve pages in all, I wrote it over the weekend.' 'That's great,' I acknowledged. 'You writing your own.' I surveyed her story. It was marvellous. But what did she reckon to mine? Joyce told me that she had only read the first few pages, 'I got fed up with it.' First, she told me that I'd got certain parts of her life story, 'Not quite right'. Second, she still did not approve of the narrative style. 'You keep repeating things,' she told me. 'If you write it, then you've got to write it like *I do.*'

### Negotiating collaboration

I asked Joyce what she thought we should do with my story. I told her that she could do whatever she wanted with it: still use it in the thesis, use bits of it, or get rid of it altogether. I reminded her that there were things she had told me in the interview that were in my story but absent in her story. She replied, 'Well, use mine and add bits from your story but *write it like I would.*' I told Joyce that I couldn't write like her. I could try but ultimately it would still be my story. She thought for a while and then suggested, 'Okay, I tell you what. Put your story first

– "Danny's story" – then "Joyce's story" after it'. This seemed like a fair compromise. I then asked her, 'What would you like to tell the reader?' Joyce's answer appeared as a statement presented before her life story in the thesis:

> Danny wrote two stories. Joyce couldn't read the first and she didn't like the second one. Joyce kept pulling Danny up, so she wrote her own. You will see that I have been going over the things Danny missed. If there's anything that I have missed that I told Danny before he wrote his story, about the centre and other things, well I'm 65 and I just kept forgetting bits. As you read my story you will see that I keep going back over the old days, when I kept remembering little things. So I would like you to read both stories (Danny's and mine) but I think you'll think mine is better.

### Stopping writing

Negotiations continued. Referring to her story she told me, 'I know I keep going back to the old days, it's just I keep adding something else I've remembered.' She told me that she was going to start keeping a diary, 'A record for the future'. Towards the end of her story I noticed that she'd written me a note:

> I know there will be a lot more to say as time goes by. I might write again soon.

I asked Joyce if this meant that she hadn't finished her story. 'For the time being anyway,' she replied. I told Joyce of my plans to start writing up my thesis, which would include her story, as soon as possible. She understood and remarked, 'I suppose I could go on writing for ever!' For the time being she was happy for me to use what she had given me at that time. Finally she wanted me to put the spelling right ('I was tired when I wrote it') and insert the last paragraph earlier into the text ('where I have spoken about Sally').

On typing up her story I kept the structure she had imposed on the text. However, in certain places punctuation and grammar were changed (full stops inserted where many commas made for a long sentence, quotation marks included and paragraphs constructed), while names were changed and titles added (e.g. 'Mr Jones' the centre manager). Joyce has told me since:

> You know I have to put things in a way that I like. I suppose that's just me.

Don't we all?

### Reflecting on part 3 – lessons from Joyce Kershaw

Joyce left me negotiating a place in the narrative inquiry. Someone else writing her story was not good enough. Comparing our stories, some of the same experiences are mentioned. It appears that my story captured a number of Joyce's experiences but I had not presented them in ways that she wanted. There are a number of lessons to be learnt. I had to discuss with Joyce about including my story in the thesis. Joyce shifted the locus of power from researcher to participant, then back to me again. My role was clarified through our discussions. However, following Sparkes (1994, p. 169), my assumption of the need for a collaborative relationship underscored my perception of Joyce as disempowered, disregarding her power to determine the nature of the relationship.

Plummer (1983, p. 106) grandly asserts that life story researchers need 'to turn to the tools of the novelist, poet and the artist'. However, to paraphrase Joyce Kershaw, narrative inquiry may benefit further by supporting informants to 'write their bloody own stories'.

## CONCLUSION

In this chapter I have outlined three stages of collaborative narrative inquiry. In Sutcliffe's (1990, p. 21) study a self-advocate urged peers, 'You must begin to tell your stories – tell people what has happened to you.' Collaborative life story research constitutes a method in which people with learning difficulties become involved in the telling of their own stories – sometimes with others, sometimes alone. By appealing to the lived and active characters of language, life stories challenge academia's reliance upon decontextualised understandings of life (Parker and Shotter, 1990). Moreover, they introduce back into what might be called academic fiction a focus on practical meaning: educating the educators about the oppressive content of ruling illusions (Marx and Engels, 1977). As Paulo Freire (1970) recognised, if oppressed people are to gain emancipation then they need to be wholly involved in the construction and doing of their own self-empowerment. One could argue that the 'special informant with learning difficulties' is a term thought-up and applied by 'experts' to a minority grouping. However, storytellers can highlight and challenge the tendency of researchers to make difficulties and differences.

## ACKNOWLEDGEMENTS

To Jackie Downer, Lloyd Page, Joyce Kershaw, Anya Souza and 'Phillip Collymore' for telling it like it is. To Kevin Fehin for discussions about materialism, Marxism and action.

## REFERENCES

Allport, G. W. (1947) *The Use of Personal Documents in Psychological Science*. New York: Social Science Research Council.
Angrosino, M. V. (1994). On the bus with Vonnie Lee: explorations in life history and metaphor. *Journal of Contemporary Ethnography*, Vol. 23 (April), pp. 14–28.

Atkinson, D. (1993) Relating, in P. Shakespeare, D. Atkinson and S. French (eds.) *Reflecting on Research Practice: Issues in Health and Social Welfare.* Buckingham: Open University Press.

Atkinson, D., and Williams, F. (eds.) (1990). *'Know Me as I am': An Anthology of Prose, Poetry and Art by People with Learning Difficulties.* Kent: Hodder & Stoughton in association with the Open University and MENCAP.

Bannister, P., Burman, E., Parker, I., Taylor, M. and Tindall, C. (1994). *Qualitative Research Methods in Psychology: A Research Guide.* Buckingham: Open University Press.

Barnes, M. (1994) Objective research or social interaction? Researching users' views of services. *Research, Policy & Planning,* Vol. 12, no. 2, pp. 1–3.

Bertaux, D. (1981). From the life history approach to the transformation of sociological practice, in D. Bertaux (ed.), *Biography and Society: the Life History Approach in the Social Sciences.* Beverly Hills: Sage.

Bertaux-Wiame, I. (1981) The life history approach to the study of internal migration, in D. Bertaux (ed.) *Biography and Society: the Life History Approach in the Social Sciences.* Beverly Hills: Sage.

Bogdan, R. and Taylor, S. (1976). The judged not the judges: an insider's view of mental retardation. *American Psychologist,* Vol. 31, pp. 47–52.

Booth, T. and Booth, W. (1994) *Parenting under Pressure: Mothers and Fathers with Learning Difficulties.* Buckingham: Open University Press.

Bruner, J. (1987) Life as narrative. *Social Research,* Vol. 54 (Spring), pp. 11–32.

Clandinin, D. J. and Connely, F. M. (1994) Personal experience methods, in N. Denzin and Y. Lincoln (eds.) *Handbook of Qualitative Research.* Thousand Oaks, CA: Sage.

Clough, P. and Barton, L. (eds.) (1995) *Making Difficulties: Research and the Construction of Special Educational Needs.* London: Paul Chapman.

Deacon, J. (1974). *Tongue Tied.* London: MENCAP.

Dexter, L. A. (1956) Towards a sociology of the mentally defective. *American Journal of Mental Deficiency,* Vol. 61, pp. 10–16.

Didion, J. (1979) *The White Album.* New York: Simon and Shuster.

Edgerton, R. B. (1984) Introduction, in R. B. Edgerton (ed.) *Lives in Process: Mentally Retarded Adults in a Large City.* Washington DC: Monograph #6 American Association on Mental Deficiency.

Ferguson, P. M., Ferguson, D. L. and Taylor, S. J. (1992) The future of interpretivism in disability studies, in P. M. Ferguson, D. L. Ferguson and S. J. Taylor (eds.) *Interpreting Disability: A Qualitative Reader.* New York: Teachers College Press.

Flynn, M. C. (1986) Adults who are mentally handicapped as consumers: issues and guidelines for interviewing. *Journal of Mental Deficiency Research,* Vol. 30, pp. 369–77).

Flynn, M. C. and Saleem, J. K. (1986). Adults who are mentally handicapped and living with their parents: satisfaction and perceptions regarding their lives and circumstances. *Journal of Mental Deficiency,* Vol. 30, pp. 379–87.

Freire, P. (1970) *Pedagogy of the Oppressed.* London: Penguin.

Gergen, K. J. and Gergen, M. M. (1988). Narrative and the self as relationship. *Advances in Experimental Psychology,* Vol. 21, pp. 17–56.

Goodley, D. (1996) Tales of hidden lives: a critical examination of life history research with people who have learning difficulties. *Disability & Society,* Vol. 11, no. 3, pp. 333–48.

Hatch, J. A. and Wisniewski, R. (eds.) (1995) *Life History and Narrative*. Lewes: Falmer Press.

Heshusius, L. (1987) Research on perceptions of sexuality by persons labelled mentally retarded, in A. Craft (ed.) *Mental Handicap and Sexuality*. Kent: Costello.

Hunt, N. (1967). *The World of Nigel Hunt*. Beaconsfield: Darwen Finlayson.

Korbin, J. E. (1986) Sarah: the life course of a Down's Syndrome child, in L. L. Langness and H. G. Levine (eds.), *Culture and Retardation*. Kluwer: D. Reidel Publishing Company.

Lather, P. (1986) Research as praxis. *Harvard Educational Review*, Vol. 56, no. 3, pp. 257–77.

Lawthom, R. (1996) You're just like my daughter: articulation of a feminist discourse. Paper presented at the Psychology of Women Conference, University of Bristol.

Lofland, J. (1971) *Analyzing Social Situations: a Guide to Qualitative Observation and Analysis*. Belmont, California: Wardsworth.

Lowe, K. and de Paiva, S. (1988). Canvassing the views of people with a mental handicap. *The Irish Journal of Psychology*, Vol. 9, no. 2, pp. 220–34.

Marx, K. (1845) Theses on Feuerbach, in K. Marx and F. Engels (eds.) (1991) *Selected Works*. Moscow: Foreign Languages Publishing House.

Marx, K. and Engels, F. (1977) *The German Ideology*. London: Lawrence & Wishart.

Mischler, E. G. (1986) The analysis of interview narratives, in T. R. Sarbin (ed.), *Narrative Psychology: The Storied Nature of Human Conduct*. New York: Praeger.

Orne, M. T. (1962) The nature of hypnosis: artefact and essence. *Journal of Abnormal & Social Psychology*, Vol. 58, pp. 277–99.

Parker, I. and Shotter, J. (eds.) (1990) *Deconstructing Social Psychology*. London: Routledge.

Parker, T. (1963) *The Unknown Citizen*. London: Hutchinson.

Plummer, K. (1983) *Documents of Life: An Introduction to the Problems and Literature of a Humanistic Method*. London: George Allen & Unwin.

Plummer, K. (1995) Life story research, in J. A. Smith, R. Harré and L. V. Langenhove (eds.), *Rethinking Methods in Psychology*. London: Sage.

Reason, P. and Hawkins, P. (1988). Storytelling as inquiry, in P. Reason (ed.) *Human Inquiry in Action: Developments in New Paradigm Research*. London: Sage.

Shakespeare, P. (1993). Performing, in P. Shakespeare, D. Atkinson, and S. French (eds.), *Reflecting on Research Practice: Issues in Health and Social Welfare*. Buckingham: Open University Press.

Sigelman, C. K., Schoenrock, C. J., Spanhel, C. L., Hromas, S. G., Winer, J. L., Budd, E. C. and Martin, P. W. (1980). Surveying mentally retarded persons: responsiveness and response validity in three samples. *American Journal of Mental Deficiency*, Vol. 84, no. 5, pp. 479–86.

Sigelman, C. K., Budd, E. C., Winer, J. L., Schoenrock, C. J. and Martin, P. W. (1982) Evaluating alternative techniques of questioning mentally retarded persons. *American Journal of Mental Deficiency*, Vol. 86, no. 5, pp. 511–18.

Simons, K. (1994) Enabling research: People with learning difficulties. *Research, Policy & Planning*, Vol. 12, no. 2, pp. 4–5.

Smith, D. (1987) The limits of positivism in social work research. *British Journal of Social Work*, Vol. 17, pp. 401–16.

Sparkes, A. C. (1994) Life histories and the issue of voice: reflections on an emerging relationship. *Qualitative Studies in Education*, Vol. 7, no. 2, pp. 165–83.

Sutcliffe, J. (1990) *Adults with Learning Difficulties: Education for Choice and Empowerment*. Leicester: The National Institute of Adult Continuing Education in association with The Open University Press.

Taylor, S. J. and Bogdan, R. (1984) *Introduction to Qualitative Research Methods: The Search for Meanings*. (2nd edn) New York: John Wiley & Sons.

Thompson, P. (1988) *The Voice of the Past: Oral History*. (2nd edn) Oxford University Press.

Tremblay, M. (1959) The key informant technique: a non-ethnographic application. *American Anthropologist*, Vol. 59, pp. 688–98.

Walker, R. (1981) On the uses of fiction in educational research (and I don't mean Cyril Burt), in D. Smetherham (ed.), *Practicing Evaluation*. Driffield: Nafferton.

Walmsley, J. (1995). Life history interviews with people with learning difficulties. *Oral History* (Spring), pp. 71–7.

Whittemore, R., Langness, L. and Koegel, P. (1986). The life history approach to mental retardation, in L. Langness and H. Levine (eds.) *Culture and Retardation*. Kluwer: D. Reidel Publishing Company.

# 10

# DIFFERENTLY ARTICULATE? SOME INDICES OF DISTURBED/ DISTURBING VOICES

## Peter Clough

There is no clear window into the inner life of a person, for any window is always filtered through the glaze of language, signs, and the process of signification. And language, in both its written and spoken forms, is always inherently unstable, in flux, and made up of the traces of other signs and symbolic statements. Hence there can never be a clear, unambiguous statement of anything, including an intention or a meaning. (Denzin, 1989, p. 14)

Many voices were raised in *Making Difficulties* (Clough and Barton, 1995) and after. The collection itself brought together – within the harmonising theme of self-conscious and self-critical enquiry – a variety of different research voices. And a number of voices responded in review of the collection, many identifying 'voice' itself as the critical issue variously at work in the volume. Dyson (1996), particularly, dwelt on voice as the most challenging motif of the book in asking the deceptively simple: 'Whose voice is being heard here?' (p. 126).

The present collection has vocalised further explorations of that question, looking amongst other things at the issues of voice (in emancipatory research) of both the researcher and the 'researched', and in terms of the 'authenticity' and validity of those voices. Various characterisations of 'voice' are adduced throughout the collection, but they gather in two main and interrelated strands: firstly, voice as a function of power (or, indeed, powerlessness); and secondly, voice as the medium for narrative expression; each of these strands may be individual or collective, and each mapped onto the other. (See, for an exemplary summary of this, Swain and French, Chapter 4 of this book.)

Above all, perhaps, for this collection 'voice' is always *contestable;* as Denzin (1989) has it, language itself is ambiguous, shifting with the event of its use. But this is something of a, perhaps, privileged view, and it has no necessary orthodoxy in social science (nor in any other field of enquiry). Elsewhere, 'voice' is not conceptualised so problematically, and may have other meanings even for those researchers occupied apparently with the same set of phenomena. For example, in a recent collection called *The Voice of the Child*, Davie, Upton and Varma (1996) bring together a number of accounts which have a common characteristic: I interpret them as sharing an overly literal understanding of 'voice' as the expression of an 'inner' identity in a legally constituted auditorium. At the heart of this conception I infer the relatively unproblematic notion of 'voice' as:

- *primarily 'knowable'* – at least partly because it is . . .
- *politically* defined only in terms of legal 'rights';
- *developmentally* understood as a function of intellectual 'growth';
- *physiologically* and *psychologically* attributable to certain stateable psycho-motor conditions;
- *empirically* accessible through technical assessment;
- *experientially* 'heard' (interpreted) as the expression of a subjective identity; and thus . . .
- *only contingently social*

For such a view, voice does not itself struggle for rights, but is disposed *after* rights are established; voice is licensed by these rights. It follows from this view that the task for research is largely one of 'turning up the volume' on the depressed or inaudible voice; this is achieved primarily through a series of policy and legislative modulations, though also by means of various technico-legal interventions thus licensed (see particularly Hall, 1996; Glaser, 1996; Ross, 1996; all in Davies *et al.* op. cit.).

But in fact, listening to subjects with special educational needs throws into a particular relief all the generically difficult issues of researching 'voice' – issues to do with *who* is listening to *whom, why* and – above all, perhaps – *in whose interests?* For, like most research subjects in the majority of studies, they are identified because they reflect – if not quite represent – a particular population; they represent the experiences of a more or less distinct category (black males, NQTs, Y8 girls, etc.); thus by definition, subjects with special educational needs are identified because they are categorically different (if not deficient). In such research they are primarily interesting, therefore, because of a perceived *difference* – however benignly understood, and however politically motivated the study.

Secondly, the research act of listening to voice must always involve the (broadly defined) processes of both mediation and translation; and again, in the case of special educational needs these functions may be particularly indicated where there are doubts about the capacity of the subject to express an intention; doubts, that is, about his or her powers of articulation.

Both these aspects are, of course, functions of the much larger question of the power-relations between the researcher and the researched. For the most part, life stories are articulated by the conventionally articulate (see Booth and Booth, 1996 for an extended discussion and bibliography). How is such advocacy justified, and at what cost? Sparkes (1994), for example, justifies such acts of writing – by people who hold advantaged positions – in terms of their more effective challenge to their privileged peers *by virtue of those positions*; he argues that studies by marginalised individuals/groups may reflect false consciousness, or may be 'coated with self-protective ideology'; and, more pragmatically, he questions whether – almost by definition – the marginalised individual possesses the resources (of various cultural capital) for effectively telling his or her own story.

For some writers, the project is thus an attempt to forge dialogical empathies between the alienated, between each of our 'othernesses' (e.g. Rorty, 1989). Thus Geertz seeks to enlarge

> the possibility of intelligible discourse between people quite different from one another in interest, outlook, wealth and power, and yet contained in a world where, tumbled as they are into endless connection, it is increasingly difficult to get out of each other's way (1988, p. 147).

But this essentially humanist (Barone, 1995) project of solidarity and empathy is not enough for some story writers (and readers), who act politically through 'storied' voice specifically to emancipate; who ultimately seek, that is, a redistribution of power. Thus the search is for the articulation of a persuasive voice which will challenge readers' interests, privileges and prejudices. As bell hooks has it, such writers can provide searing, harrowing 'chronicles of pain' – though she reminds us that these may well serve merely to 'keep in place existing structures of domination' (1991, p. 59) if they do not bring about a deep unease in the reader.

How should we bring unease about? Michel Butor (1970) was writing of the novelist (but I insist that he really meant 'the educational researcher'!) when he wrote

> The novelist who refuses to accept this task [of 'unmasking, exploration, and adaptation'] never discarding old habits, never demanding any particular effort of his reader, never obliging him to confront himself, to question attitudes long since taken for granted . . . becomes the accomplice of that profound uneasiness, that darkness, in which we are groping our way. He stiffens the reflexes of our consciousness even more, making any awakening more difficult; he contributes to its suffocation, so that even if his intentions are generous, his work is in the last analysis a poison . . .

What follows is another attempt (see Clough, 1995, 1996) to dispose empirical data as a persuasive art which challenges some of the above notions of voice and learning difficulty. But, as you will read, such an attempt to articulate in this way is not without difficulty.

*

This is a story of boys, teachers and a school with difficulties. It's a story used to express the difficulties of articulating difficulties, and the difficulties of those who are *differently articulate*. The chapter is built around a story which I put together five years after my involvement with a school which I have described elsewhere as

> of great interest: a big (about 2,000 students) place fairly downtown in a big city tired with industrial collapse; fitfully tense – in this retrenchment – with a substantial Pakistani community brought so many years ago thousands of miles indifferently as so many operatives; and made slightly famous by local politicians who polarised each other into caricatures of left and right (one Labour councillor described the Tory leader – in his presence – as *'itler wi' knobs on'*; this without a smile). (Clough, 1995, p. 132)

My broad project to understand the culture of 'special' education in that school is described there, too (ibid., pp. 141–2), but this particular story is knit from my more specific attempts in that school to get a handle on the 'bad lads', where resistance – being bad – called for some flair on the part of white lads in a school 94 per cent populated by Asian – and a handful of African-Caribbean – kids.

The story is an amalgm of raw transcribed observation, interview events, notes of conversations, my own research journal and imports of my own knowing and belief. It demands much of those who read it. We struggle to make sense of the situations we witness, read of, participate in – and we are discomforted by the struggle. So, in this story, you – as a reader of knots of difficulty in the life of this school, these teachers and these boys – must weave together your own fabric to make sense of the data I provide. It is difficult work – dealing with difficulty is so. Life events sometimes unfold for an individual in a difficult order, pieces of understanding hang for a while in consciousness and experience – waiting for a connection – waiting for meaning – sometimes finding none. Such is *A story of Molly*.

My story of difficulty is ever so slightly knit with what Yalom (1989) calls *'symbolically equivalent substitutes'* to be sure of anonymity. As to method, I have my own struggle to understand it and remain (still) one story ahead of making my method.[1] In the case of this particular story, I owe something to George Riseborough for his 'GBH; the Gobbo Barmy Army' (Riseborough, 1993) which is one of the most horrid things I've ever read; an incredible achievement, but horrid.

I should issue another warning – at this, the watershed hour – that there are some horrid things in this story, too – difficult to write and (I am told)

---

[1] As to method generally, I owe much to the work of Tim Booth, Wendy Booth, Barbara Cole, Jenny Corbett, Danny Goodley, Ivor Goodson, Pat Sykes, Andrew Sparkes, Margarete Sandelowski, and of course to the Bertaux, Denzins, Faradays and Plummers who assembled the larger timbers.

difficult to read. But I believe they only narrowly disguise more truly horrid things. There are in this story many of the difficulties of inequality which pervade much of education, and which are especially entangled in any discussion of children with difficulties. Throughout the story you will find issues of endemic racism bound up with clashes of culture and struggles of the working class and unemployed. Young people – born British – are still maligned for their origins, and their abilities to speak two (or more) languages either go unnoticed or – worse – are a source of ridicule.

And this is a story mainly about boys, the kinds of boys who make up the 1 in 12 who leave school with no GCSE passes (DfEE, 1997a, p. 79). They are boys who have not achieved what school wanted of them; boys who might not have known what they wanted of themselves; and boys who – for reasons I do not propose to discuss here – could or would not achieve what their families wanted of them. In 1996, 48 per cent of 14-year-old boys scored level 5 or above in National Curriculum tests; for girls the figure was 66 per cent (DfEE, 1997a). Boys' underachievement in English set alarm bells ringing again. Low achievement in English – we should say literacy – inhibits a great deal of the curriculum, and pupils may well experience struggle in each aspect of the curriculum. In 1997 national strategies were put in place to address issues of underachievement with a government White Paper on Education (DfEE, 1997a) *Excellence in Schools* closely followed by a Green Paper (DfEE, 1997b) which set the tone for consultation on future government policy on Special Educational Needs. The White Paper stated:

> Education is the key to creating a society which is dynamic and productive, offering opportunity and fairness to all. It is the Government's top priority. We will work in partnership with all those who share our passion and sense of urgency for higher standards. (DfEE, 1997a, p. 9)

For the boys in this story – and for Molly especially – there was no such opportunity, no such creativity – only blame and expectation of continued and increasingly complex difficulties – perpetual undesirable behaviour. There was passion – running deep – but it was not a passion for lessons or learning; it was a passion driven by survival.

## A STORY OF MOLLY

Tim Booth asked me: 'How do you give a voice to people who lack words?'

My problem with Molly is not that he *lacks* words, but rather that they can spill out of him with a wild, fairground pulse; they are sparklers, he waves them splashing around him. And my other problem with Molly's words is that many of them are not very nice; they are squibs that make you jump out of the way. For the moment I think that these are my only problems.

I have been sitting with Molly for some ten minutes and he has explained why the pond at Tenby Dale has been closed for restocking. The tale is so parochial, has such artless warmth and polish that I feel that Molly and I are like something out of *Kes*. I think I am quite skilled at not patronising the Mollies, so I don't entirely aspirate my h's, but I think that Molly will know somehow that I'm alright; or 'o'reet' I would want him to say to his mates; *'e's o'reet that researcher bloke – 'im wi t'leather jacket'* But at this, my first meeting with Molly, I am unprepared for the sudden lash that I later come to know him by. So – and God knows where this comes from – I find myself of a moment saying – 'Look here, Molly: you're intelligent, you're bright, you could' . . . and I don't finish my sentence before Molly raps: 'What an' become a twat like thee? No offence but common sense/self-defence/off-a dat fence what? – what?,

And my audience with Molly is over for today. He is already on his feet and moving *through*, somehow, rather than round, the desks between him and the door. No longer Billy Casper, he is become Anthony Burgess's – Alex? – of *Clockwork Orange* – *Widdy-widdy-widdy-boom-boom*, and his hands beat a tattoo on the desks as he passes them. *Widdy-widdy-widdy*.

I notice that I am disappointed at being called a twat.

*

Molly is fifteen years old, nearly sixteen when I meet him. His face bears traces of a prettiness that he will soon properly lose as his complexion yields fully to adolescence; for the moment, though, let him still be pretty, though his voice is at odds: mostly broken (though still sometimes – in excitement, I come to learn – there are light flecks in with the gravel).

His name is Francis Molinetti, and there are a number of reasons why I appear to pick him out from John Francis (Tosser), Des Bailey, Tom McPhee (Toffee) and a host of indifferent others. The first of these reasons – when I think about it – has to have something to do with Molly's brightness. You can see this in his face, but not in *this* sort of brow, *that* sort of nose, or a sparkling eye, or any such. Unless it closes down – and just occasionally it does – this face is simply open with mirth. At nine he would have looked mischievous; at fifteen he is not yet watchful – though this will surely come later, after careful and before baleful; these things, too, are written in his face – no, he is not yet watchful so much as alert to possibility.

When I visit his home to meet his mother, I am amused by the identical downy moustache that they share. With her, his face loses all its nascent adult shapes, and becomes in all sincerity an artless peasant – Mario Rapuello, say – as he gazes at her with love and – not at all shy in my presence – ducks and recoils with glee from her softly cuffing him.

'Wha' ah do, eh?*(cuff)* 'Ah buy 'im a bice! Eh? *(cuff)* 'Ah buy 'im a bice an' wha' 'e do, eh? *(cuff)* 'E *(cuff)* sell *(cuff)* 'e! 'E sell 'e!'

I think that Mrs Molinetti has at some point bought Molly a bike, which he has sold. Molly, however, is full of glee; he is a young boy laughing, an old man crying, and she pulls his head onto her bosom, and even this does not compromise his joy at the scolding.

I bought him a bike. *Bice* might be a good try under other circumstances, except that Mrs Molinetti has been in England for nearly fifty years, and has roughly knit a patois – threads of West Yorkshire across a stronger, Milanese yarn – which serves her sufficiently to deal with the cone-salesmen and the women on the market. Otherwise, it seems, she has little need of English, for her family is plentiful in this city.

'Wha' you goin' do wi' 'im, eh? 'E goes a Youth [club] in a new trouse, 'e comes 'ome in a jean is not 'is, eh? So where you trouse, eh? I say him: Franny where you trouse, eh? He say: "ah don't know mam". [*ah doornt naw mam*].'

Molly is delighted with this telling off, and I am again surprised at his ease in this revelation to me.

'Wha' we goin' do wi' 'im, eh?'

She looks at him as he is the most beautiful and successful man she has ever known; and he looks up in a rueful cliché at her through his long eyelashes. I witness this freight – between man and woman – with some embarrassment. I am here because I want to know how Molly's family are dealing with his exclusion from school, but it is now clear not only that Mrs Molinetti doesn't know he is excluded – and how has he managed that one? – but that in any event we should not have been able to find a shared tongue to pass either the time of day or judgement on Molly.

As Molly is seeing me to the door, I say 'She doesn't know, does she?' and Molly smiles and looks me full in the eye.

[*I am back in the school on Wednesday, and when I go to Time Out, Tosser, Des, Toffee and Mong are vicious*]

'Tha'rt a snake, thee,' says Des, pointing a charged contempt down his finger at me.
'Fuckin' snake', adds Mong.

(The teacher – whom I have not seen before – makes a limp effort at quietening the boys, but may as well not be there. I start to explain who I am, but realise that she doesn't want or need to know.)

'Tha' stuffed 'im reet, tha' did.'

'We ain't talkin' to thee no more.'

'Tha'rt a snake, thee,' adds Mong, looking to affiliate with this choler; but draws instead a phlegm to himself; Toffee hawks and gobs directly onto Mong's workbook.

'Shut tha' fuckin' gob Mong.'

Des throws a full-sized clay model football boot at Mong, which hits him behind his ear (though does not break until it hits the floor).

'They're not normally like this . . .' the teacher starts feebly, taking me for – what? – an inspector?

[A pause in the telling now. This is a difficult story to tell and to read. It seems that this particular 'chronicle of pain' is in danger of keeping in place those 'existing structures of dominion' of which bell hooks warned. For, in the final analysis, I lack permission – from myself and my publishers – to continue to tell the story here in quite this way. To write (and read) *fuckin'* once or twice might (might) be OK – it is a quotation from a transcript gleaned from empirical work after all. But the parameters set for us (and to some extent *by* us) form 'nets' to our work which constrain us – and act to inhibit the harshest of voices. We have made our nets of methods which have a large enough mesh to let through much of the catches trawled from our research data but which are still not large enough to let through those things which will destroy our selves or our work.

So the story as you will read it now is not the story I wrote and sent to the publishers of this book. That version was closer to the voices – the language – of those characters in the story than the version you will read. But it has been inhibited. It did not fit within the boundaries of what one can write in an academic text (and still remain a member of a research community). The story you will read is still a horrid tale, but from here on I will cut and trim the language, though on some occasions I will risk pushing at the parameters because I will not deny, for example, the racist terms which sting.]

Gin finds me out at lunchtime as I am leaving the staff room.
'Sir . . . '
'Don't call me sir, Gin'.
'Molly, sir. 'Is brother beat 'im up after you'd been, Monday. It's why he's not 'ere today, 'e shoulda been back today, right? Lol, Lolly. Beat 'im up reet, 'as a face like mince beef, sir.'
'Lol?'
'Lolly's 'is brother, sir. Runs the business. 'As a personal number plate.'

[The head of the business – Molly's eldest brother by seventeen years – is called Lolly; not, actually, because it is an Ice Cream business, but because he was christened Lorenzo]

*

| | |
|---|---|
| Molly | It's the only language 'e 'ad. It's the only thing 'e knew. Wham! Bang! Lol's the same. |
| PC | Lol? |
| M | Lolly, me brother Lolly. Language of the fist. Smack first, ask later. |
| PC | Does Lol . . . did Lol get it? I mean when he was little. |
| M | Oh God, ay. When 'e was big, too – eighteen, nineteen. I've seen 'im push Lol through the shed door. Lol came back [*from a day's ice-cream van round*] 60p down or something, and 'e just smacked him – wham! – and he went through't shed door. Not as much as me, though. 'E 'ated me cos I could speak, I used to speak . . . |
| PC | How d'you mean 'speak'? |
| M | I used to answer 'im back. Like 'e'd say: You think you're so bloody smart, eh? An' I'd say summat like [*in mock-posh voice*]: 'I'm reasonably well-provided for above the neck, father' – an' e'd go bloody bonkers – Wham! Wham! Smack-bloody-smack! |
| PC | What . . . you mean you knew? That he'd hit you? |
| M | Yeh, course. It was my only defence against him – words, 'e 'ated words, me dad did, 'ated 'em. |
| PC | So you wound him up with words . . . and he'd then hit you? |
| M | Something like that. Yeh, summat like that. |
| PC | Why? |
| M | [*after a long pause . . . 10 seconds?*] Survival? [*Appears to think about this; then:*] Yeh: survival. I learned to lie to survive. |

\*

A week or so later he stops me in the corridor and thrusts a paper at me and it's torn from a Penguin school poetry anthology. 'That's a bit what it was, what it was like. He mutters (without lips) and is gone and within seconds I can hear him way down the corridor, become Alex again: *Widdy-widdy-widdy* . . .
The torn page is Ephraim Moras' 'Bowl of Fruit':

a small child, less than table-height,
is reaching for an apple on the table;
every time his fingers near the apple, a fist smashes down on his fingers;

one time he touches the apple even,
and the fist smashes him in the face,
sending his head hard against the architrave behind him.

From the floor a theory of apples starts like this.

\*

*[Mr Desborough is 51 and is Deputy Headteacher]*

D   We are talking one nasty piece of work, just that: a nasty piece of work.
PC   Was he always, I mean when?
D   Something happens. His first year he was alright. Obscure but alright. I'll tell you what, though, we take all the Y9 to the Lakes at Easter, well Carlisle but. Molinetti shat in a staff sleeping bag
PC   Shat?
D   We were all out for the evening, a sort of wide game, you know and he came back to the huts and he shat, he deliberately, well you couldn't accidentally he actually went in one of the staff huts, he shat in this, in Mark's sleeping bag. Had rolled it down, shat, zipped it back up, put the pillow job back. Mark gets into bed, I was there, wriggles down – yeugggh!
PC   Mark Hedley? What did you do/how was he dealt with?
D   Oh there was no proof, we couldn't do anything. Short of having a path lab report on the turd, you couldn't prove anything. But you see he would know that, Molinetti, oh we're dealing with a clever one here make no mistake.
PC   Ah but he *is* clever isn't he? I think he . . .
D   No not really. He's not really clever. He's learned a few tricks is all, a few tricks of language it's true he has it's true. Have you spoken to Mark, Mark Hedley? Yeh? Well Mark will tell you, he's told you I'm sure, that Molinetti is a misunderstood . . . a misunderstood *hero*, Molinetti is a bad lot is all, I'm afraid. One bad lot.
PC   Yeh, Mark does think a lot of him
D   D'you know what Molinetti thinks of Mark? Mark who champions him, St Mark who, look, this is between us, but Mark who'd, no I can say it, I can, I'll own to it . . . Mark has this thing about reaching out to kids, speaking but really speaking to them and Molinetti plays him like a kite, like a kite. Mark refused to believe that it was Molinetti shat in his sleeping bag, wouldn't have it. Now ask yourself, ask me, ask *why* would

Molinetti shit in Hedley's sleeping bag? Answer that, eh? Well, I'll tell
you, he was appalled he was just *appalled* to be championed by a fag . . .
he was just appalled it's as simple as that.

[*Two days later; 10.45 a.m.; Molly and the other boys are waiting in 'Time Out'
for Mr Stephenson*]

| | |
|---|---|
| Molly | Ilkley: what a f*****' place to grow up in, eh? Ave yer ever bin? I tell yer. |
| Gin | 'Arrogate. |
| Des | F*****' 'arrogate. |
| Gin | York. |
| Des | F*****' York. |
| Gin | Whitby. |
| Des | F*****' Shitby. |

[*laughter; inaudible*]

| | |
|---|---|
| M | Near this joke-shop, reet *(right)*? and traffic-warden, Paki reet? says [*in caricatured pan-Asian dialect:*] 'You must not be parrr-king here, oh no, oh my goodness gracious no, innit?' Reet? 'n our Lol, reet? he says |

[*Noise/chaos as Des falls backwards off desk*]

| | |
|---|---|
| Des | Tha' pushed me f***-face. |
| Gin | Ah f*****' didn't |
| Des | Tha' f*****' did, tha' f*****' dees *(dies)* thee, tha' does, tha' f*****' wait . . . |

It goes on; it goes on and on; it goes on and on and on and how it wearies; its tired,
routine ugliness actually makes you tired; it sucks the life from the room.

 Mr Stephenson enters. He knows I'm with the boys and (correctly) ignores me.
The boys sort-of stand.

| | |
|---|---|
| Mr S | Sit down, lads. What happened/Don't all talk at once. Ginner? |
| Gin | I weren't even there, Sir. |
| Molly | 'E weren't. Sir, somebody put it in his bag. |
| Mr S | Shut up for a minute, Molinetti. |
| Molly | But 'e weren't, Sir, it's not just. |
| Mr S | Just, Molly? Tell me about justice, then. |
| Molly | Sir it's not right, Govinder did it 'n put it in Gin's bag, Sir, it's always the same if it's a Paki. Sir. |
| Mr S | D'you want to think about what you just said, Molinetti? |
| Molly | No sir, it's true sir, t'Pakis always get away wi' it. |
| Mr S | Right, Molinetti and Ginner stay here, the rest of you get off to class. |

(*Turning to me:*) I wonder if you'd mind leaving us as well?

*

[*Mark Hedley: second-in-command SEN*]

Mark Hedley says 'Ooh, that Salma Fariq! Ooh,' he says, 'ooh. she's awful!' And
his wrist flops away to the right as his head tosses to the left with the slightest 'ter'.
I can't believe this the first time I meet him, and he excites in me a dismissive scorn.
He is five feet four – no more – and dressed top to toe in black, trailing the fashion
by a few years, but making a strong point for all that. His shirt is black with a very

narrow charcoal tie. He has two tiny silver sleepers in each of his ears.

MH    It's 'cos I look young, I do have some difficulties, but then I don't too, if you know what I mean. I get on very well – very well – with children who have problems both academically and otherwise socially. I get on very well for some reason with the roughs, the very badly behaved, I get on with them very well indeed. I get satisfaction from watching them achieve something that they wouldn't otherwise.

PC    If someone stood back and looked at what you were doing what would they say was happening? What would they identify . . . as the things that made it possible for you to get on well with those . . .

MH    Tough guys and

PC    Yeh

MH    I think one of the reasons I get on with them is because I was exactly the same when I was at school. I was expelled from school because of my behaviour and stuff and I'm still quite young [26] and I can identify still with what's going on. I know how I was treated at school but there's no way, there's no way that I would ever treat anybody in the same way . . . . . . the school I went to, I mean the whole attitude of the place stank as far as I was concerned. The teachers were appalling. If they came to a school like this they'd be dead within a week because they couldn't actually teach. I got picked on a lot, I can't tell you how awful it was. *Aw*ful! One teacher used to hide behind the door and when I used to come in the room he used to grab me and put me out the window because there was a ledge on the window and he used to make me sit outside the window. It was *aw*ful.

PC    That's appalling! I take it that was on the ground floor . . .

MHH   No, it was the second floor..

*[Later]*

M     Well I've never been one to take things easily if I don't agree. I'm quite an independent person and I just started acting up all the time and being really destructive, did no work, I was a punk and all this sort of thing. I died my hair, wouldn't wear school uniform, all that sort of thing, in the end they just asked me to go, much to my mother's *ut*ter dismay and horror. Then I came here and loved it and settled in straight away.

PC    What, you came to this school?

MH    Yeh, I . . .

PC    I mean – as a pupil?

MH    Yes I came into the fifth year.

PC    Wow . . . I . . .

MH    And it's part of why I get on with the kids, 'cos I know what it's like both sides of the fence, you know? And I am still young, that's important.

PC    You said that before, is it very important to you, that?

MH    Oh yes, oh yes, yes. I think here with me being quite young looking I find that pupils – not just from my own form but from other forms as well – they just come and chat and talk either about a problem or they'll just come for a chat or a joke. I find that really helps being young and . . . sometimes I find I'm in a bit of an awkward position because they are trying to get me to side with them against other teachers and stuff and that's really difficult, especially when I agree with what they're saying. I find that happens quite a lot.

PC　　Does anyone get upset about your dress, the way you dress?

MH　　Oh I'm surprised I've not been sacked! I'm quite happy with what I am, it works well for me and I get through to the kids which is the most important.

PC　　Do you feel any criticism, any explicit criticism of how you look, how you dress, what you are, whatever . . .

MH　　Yes from some people. I wear the ear-rings, funny shoes perhaps. Some people would probably think it's not a suitable way for a teacher to look. But me . . . well, I'd rather be around the kids, anyway. I would say that the people I empathise most with here are the children. That sounds a bit corny I know but I'd much rather be with them than the staff most of the time. I still feel young at heart, that's another corny thing to say but I still feel very youthful. There're lots of ways I feel very old too but I like to sit down and talk about music and stuff and I think what kids do is exciting and what they are is exciting and you see all the potential in them. I think I've made a lot of mistakes in my life and I don't want them to do the same, the same sort of things.

*[Later/another day]*

M　　I don't really judge kids you see, I get angry if I'm rubbed up the wrong way but the kids know I'm not going to go apeshit. Like the other day when [Head of Science] sent a child, Molinetti to me.

PC　　Ah, Molly!

MH　　You've met Molly, Molly's great, fierce, fiercely bright.

PC　　How do you get on with Molly? Does Molly . . .

MH　　He's me is Molly, just like me, we're like two animals sort of sniffing round each other, mutual respect, he wouldn't come too close but he wouldn't stay too far away, he . . .

PC　　Why was he sent to you?

MH　　. . . knows his boundaries. Oh [science teacher] can't stand kids as bright as himself, I don't know, Molly said something. I mean, fancy a fifty-year old-man having to send a fifteen-year-old child to a twenty-six year-old form tutor because he was cheeky!

PC　　What did you do, to Molly?

MH　　Oh talked to him, then there's a procedure, he had to go to Time Out for the rest of the morning.

*[Later]*

M　　I always try to treat people how I'd want them to treat me. I wouldn't expect anybody to tell me how to behave or what to do or what to think so I wouldn't do that to other people. I expect kids to be treated in the same way as . . . well, how I treat adults. You've got to give them the same sort of responsibilities . . . I think there is an awful tendency when you're working with youngsters to treat them in a very condescending way and treat them as children. Yes they are young people and they haven't got your wealth of experience but I just think they are the same really. I mean, I think I've got . . . I don't like talking this way because it sounds like you're blowing your own trumpet but I get on very easily with children and I've got a very, I think it's a very unique way of teaching, of interacting with kids. I think it's a very unique way of teaching, of interacting. I mean Molly's a classic example . . .

PC  Tell me about Molly . . .

MH  Molly's a delight. Like I say, Molly's me. Bright as a button.

*

[*I 'interview' Molly*]

M   Where shall I start?

PC  Did you have trouble at [primary school]?

M   No, not much.

PC  Not much?

M   No. Not much.

PC  Like how much?

M   Not much.

PC  Like . . . what? What did you do? Get in trouble for?

M   [*Deadpan*] I set fire to the cleaners.

PC  The cleaner's . . . what?

M   The cleaners, there were two cleaners and they were 'avin' a fag

PC  You set fire . . .

M   In this den, right? Caretaker's den, right?

PC  You mean to the cleaners themselves?

M   [*ploughing on regardless* . . . ] 'n' I set fire to this waste-paper basket, right 'n' it all went up . . . brrrrrumppphhh! [*from clasped hands, mimes the centrifugal explosion, and rolls a growling crescendo in his throat before the big, big labial plosive; he likes this effect, and repeats it, improving his performance, and then a third time, hands finally high above his head configuring dancing flames* . . . ]

PC  [*eventually, and laughing; possibly too much*] Gosh! Wow, some event, eh? And were the cleaners in the room, the den?

M   Don't be f*****' soft.

[*A long silence; maybe nearly a half minute*]

PC  I got into some right scrapes when I was at school . . .

[*Silence; Molly straightfaced now, watching through the window the soccer on the field.*]

PC  D'you want to, shall we leave it for today, then?

[*Silence; Molly suddenly bangs the window hard with his forefinger several times*]

M   [*Shouting*] Pass the f*****' thing! Pass it! Pass it! Pass it! Oh f***, Anderson! [*As player is – easily – dispossessed, 'Anderson' immediately picks up a small clod of mud and throws it towards 'our' window. It misses, but* . . . ]

The scene takes on *Kes* again; for the small, tubby middle-aged Brian Glover of a teacher who is the referee runs shouting towards us . . .

PE  Molinetti! Molinetti! Open that window! Now, Molinetti! [*He sees me and says, no jot less quietly:*] He's with you is he?

PC    Yes, I'm . . .

PE    He's with you, right, right Molinetti. [*Word by word pushed with his forefinger almost up to Molly's nose:*] KEEP-YOUR-BIG-ITALIAN-NOSE-OUT.

M    Racist, sir, that's racist, you 'eard 'im didn't yer?, racist

For a moment, a tiny moment, the PE man is quite without doubt going to seize Molly by something; doesn't, in fact, because – true to this film-script we seem to be making here – his class is now alert to the show and is in tumult.

Class    Molly! Eye-tie-shite-eye! 'Oo's yer friend in the leathers, Molly? [*Which is me.*] Molinetti wanker! Molly's gorra friend . . .

M    [*Shouting inches from 'Mr Glover's' ear*] Tha' dees *(dies)*, Pitcher, tha' f*****' dees! 'Ah'll f*****' take thee out . . .

PE    Right, Molinetti, Molinetti go on, get to the Head, go on – to the Head, no, Molinetti, that's enough, go on, now, Molinetti, go on

M    You're f*****' dead, Pitcher

PE    [*Raising a leg onto the windowsill*] Go on! Go on Molinetti! I said to the Head Molinetti. [*Climbing through the window, even!*] That's it go on! Go on! [*He is through the window and is pushing Molly; gently, but pushing. Molly catches the untied lace of a trainer beneath the other foot, and stumbling, raises a hand to right himself. Mr Glover steps back in alarm; and to me:*] You saw him! You saw that! You've done it now Molinetti! You've done it now.

And to my strange delight, Molly – seeing the gallows before him anyway, appears to think: alright – I might as well take something with me; and pops Glover neatly on the nose. Glover drops quite simply, though squealing.

    Though such an event is rehearsed in a myriad schools daily, for Molly's career this is a new turn.

*

[Two days later; waiting at the bus-stop. The excluded Molly has come to meet his mates at the gates.]

Tosser    Is it on?

PC    Yes it's on.

T    Can I say owt?

PC    If you want, but . . .

T    F***! F***-f***-f***-f***-! S*****sh**ear**f***-w***k!

Gin    Tha'rt sad, thee, Tosser.

Toffee    Play it back, sir, go on play it back.

PC    It's . . . OK. [*rewinds tape, and replays*]

Gin    Tha' sounds like a girl, thee! [*Mimics in falsetto:*] f***-f***-f***- [*etc.*]

Molly    Tha'rt the f***** girl, pin-p***k. Tha' could sh** a louse tha could.

Toff    'Ere: tha' knows Netto reet? Well Netto reckons Gin sh*** Fatima, reet?

Gin    [*Laughing*] F*****' didn't. [*Turning to Mong*] Tha' sh**s geese, dun' tha' Mong?

[*Group 'turns' to Mong*]

Mong    Goose gobbles 'im more like. [*Seizes microphone from my hand, and
        starts a whispered and minutely accurate David Attenborough imitation:*]
        Here we see the . . . baby Mong, *Mongo Mongo*, the infant Mong . . .
        under some considerable threat from . . . the other animals . . . I can see
        the adult Tosser there, *Tossus Tossus* . . . [*The others are trying to force
        Mong's head down to a dog turd on the pavement*] But wait, wait! The
        Researcher – a fine beast in his leather jacket, the corduroy trouser . . . in
        green/a *dark* green/yes – the Researcher is approaching! What law . . .
        what . . . ancient . . . law of the jungle is at work here? The bold . . . the
        . . . *manly* researcher . . . oh! He *rescues* the infant Mong! Oh what a *fine*
        beast this is! [*etc.*]

*

Karen couldn't stand working – as Research Assistant – on the project and left
as soon as she could get a 'real' job. But she kept in touch with Mark – really
liked him – and I think they 'did' clubs and things. Anyway when I saw her last
year, she told me this story: Mark and two – women – friends were crossing
Halifax Lane at about one in the morning, Sunday morning, they'd been to a
club or something and were walking down into town in search of something to
eat. Of three lads some fifty yards behind them, one started calling: 'Oy queer/
oy b\*\*boy/oy you f\*\*\*\*\*\* qu\*\*r/oy f\*\*\*-\*\*se.' His friends seemed to try to
quiet him. Mark and the women walked on, and the man called on and on.
'F\*\*\*-\*\*se/B\*\*\*\*\*\*\*b/Pervert.' The man suddenly detached himself from his
friends, who turned a corner and were gone; the man ran hard up to Mark
from behind and pushed him round. 'Ent tha gonna say nowt sh\*\*-\*\*se? Eh?
As tha nowt to say for theesen pervert?' The man rolled a gob of phlegm in his
throat – slowly, clearly – and then shot it hard onto Mark's face, where it hit
on the corner of his mouth. One of the women punched – or made to punch –
the man in his face but was too slow; he kicked her legs from under her and
stamped on her as she fell beneath him; and then he beat up the three of them,
swiftly and wildly. They lay almost without moving on the pavement for some
whole minutes before a car stopped and help was sent for.
    At the hospital the police were keen to take statements but Mark and the
women were silent and would say nothing; the police were formally polite at
first and finally – convinced that Mark knew but was protecting his attacker –
derisive. They threw the fag and his dykes out at 3.40 a.m.

\* \* \* \* \*

## CONCLUSION: SOME INHIBITED VOICES AND THE IMPASSE OF POLICY

Finding a language for working through these hunches is difficult. What you
have read here is clearly no great story; it is rather – to return to Burgess (1962,
incidentally) and *A Clockwork Orange* – at once 'a work too didactic to be
artistic' and 'art dragged into the arena of morality' (Morrison, 1996). But as a

'reflexive project of the self' (Giddens, 1991) it perhaps casts some light. Others who read a draft of this story, said it depicts many struggles; the struggles of characters looking in different directions, where sometimes gazes collide, suffering intermittently from periods of seeming blindness. The researcher – they say – battles to locate himself in his relationship with his subjects. The teachers make stabbing attempts at negotiating a discourse with each other and their pupils. The boys spar amongst themselves, vying for macho supremacy and wit, against a background of familial brutishness. It is a tragic soap opera which brings together so many discordant voices in a chorus of protest about the impossible roles that society situates them to play. The actors struggle with each other, use scripts from different plays, sometimes communicating, sometimes not.

Schools are arenas which tantalise researchers with their richness. There is so much to see, bringing revelations of the tasks which lie ahead for practitioners. Chris Woodhead (1997) reminds us of the cost of this research: 'Around £63 million of taxpayers' money is spent each year on educational research'.

Her Majesty's Chief Inspector of Schools expressed dismay at the poor value for money of some research, in terms of improving the quality of teaching – an apparent attempt to inhibit the sociological in educational research. But as *A story of Molly* illustrates, so much of what goes wrong for young people in schools is symptomatic of whole chains of events and social intricacies, so that practitioners find themselves able only to tinker frustratedly on the periphery of chasms of inequality. Just as the story (and the telling) represents sore difficulties, teachers too lack voice in telling their stories of difficulties – their language is being eroded and a new language of the state in education is being – it seems systematically – imposed. Teachers interact with young people who express as many varieties of social and cultural value as there are individuals. Moreover, the point which Woodhead ignores, is that research sometimes suggests a change in the school curriculum; this is currently beyond the remit of teachers in England and Wales, a present impasse.

So, when Tim Booth asks me again : *How do you give a voice to people who lack words?* I shall respond with my own questions:

*How do we give voice to those – the differently articulate – whose words will not be heard?*
*How do we understand that which is suppressed?*
*How do we unblock the impasse?*

## ACKNOWLEDGEMENTS

'David Desborough' is dead; 'Molly' died quite recently joy-riding in a stolen car – with kids some five years younger. 'Mark Hedley' has read and approved my story with minor amendments. 'Mr Glover' I can't get hold of, but, wherever you are: it's not really you!

Felicity Armstrong, Julia Davies, Susy Harris, David Hyatt, Jon Nixon, Cathy Nutbrown, Alan Skelton and Mairtin Mac an Ghaill read the story and said variously interesting things.

# REFERENCES

Barone, T. (1995) Persuasive writings, vigilant readings and reconstructed characters: the paradox of trust in educational storytelling, in J. Hatch and R. Wisniewski (eds.) *Life History and Narrative*. London: Falmer.

Booth, T. (1996) Sounds of still voices: issues in the use of narrative methods with people who have learning difficulties, in L. Barton, (ed.) *Disability and Society*, London: Longman.

Booth, T. and Booth, W. (1996). Sounds of silence: narrative research with inarticulate subjects. *Disability and Society*, Vol. 11, no. 1, pp. 55–70.

Butor, M. (1979) *Inventory: Essays* London: Jonathon Cape.

Clough, P. (1995) Problems of identity and method in the investigation of SEN, in Clough and Barton (*op. cit.*).

Clough, P. (1996) 'Again fathers and sons': the mutual construction of self, story and SEN. *Disability and Society*, Vol. 112, no. 1, pp. 71–81.

Clough, P. and Barton, L. (eds.) *Making Difficulties: Research and the Construction of Special Educational Needs*. London: Paul Chapman.

Coates, J. (1986) *Women, Men and Language*. London: Longman.

Davie, R., Upton, G. and Varma, V. (eds.) (1996) *The Voice of the Child*. London: Falmer.

Denzin, N. (1989) *Interpretive Interactionism*. Newbury Parl, CE: Sage.

DfEE (1997a) *Excellence in Schools*. London: HMSO.

Dyson A., (1996) Review of *Making Difficulties*. *Cambridge Journal of Education*, Vol. 26, no. 1.

Geertz, C. (1988) *Works and Lives: the Anthropologist as Author*. Stanford, CA: Stanford University Press.

Giddens, A. (1991) *Modernity and Self-Identity*. Cambridge: Polity Press.

Hall, N. (1996) Eliciting Children's Views: the Contribution of Psychologists, in Davie, R. et al (1996).

Glaser, D. (1996) The Voice of the Child in Mental Health Practice, in Davie, R. et al (1996).

hooks, bell (1991) Narratives of struggle, in P. Mariani (ed.) *Critical Fictions: the Politics of Imaginative Writing*. Seattle: Bay.

Mac an Ghaill, M. (1994) *The Making of Men*. Buckingham: Open University Press.

Mahony, P. (1985) *Schools for the Boys*. London: Hutchinson.

Morrison, B. (1996) Introduction to Burgess, A. (1962) *A Clockwork Orange*. Harmondsworth: Penguin.

Riseborough, G. (1993) GBH: The Gobbo Barmy Army, in I. Bates and G. Riseborough (eds.) *Youth and Inequality*. Milton Keynes: Open University Press.

Rorty, R. (1989) *Contingency, Irony and Solidarity*. Cambridge: Cambridge University Press.

Ross, E. M. (1996) Learning to Listen to Children, in Davie, R. et al (1996).

Sparkes, A. (1994) Life histories and the issue of voice: reflections on an emerging relationship. *International Journal of Qualitative Studies in Education*, Vol. 7, pp. 165–83

Woodhead, C. (1998) A review of sociology of education. *The New Statesman*, 20 March, p. 51.

Yalom, I. (1991) *Love's Executioner and Other Tales of Psychotherapy*. London: Penguin.

# INDEX